T0244363

About Island Press

Since 1984, the nonprofit organization Island Press has been stimulating, shaping, and communicating ideas that are essential for solving environmental problems worldwide. With more than 1,000 titles in print and some 30 new releases each year, we are the nation's leading publisher on environmental issues. We identify innovative thinkers and emerging trends in the environmental field. We work with world-renowned experts and authors to develop cross-disciplinary solutions to environmental challenges.

Island Press designs and executes educational campaigns, in conjunction with our authors, to communicate their critical messages in print, in person, and online using the latest technologies, innovative programs, and the media. Our goal is to reach targeted audiences—scientists, policy makers, environmental advocates, urban planners, the media, and concerned citizens—with information that can be used to create the framework for long-term ecological health and human well-being.

Island Press gratefully acknowledges major support from The Bobolink Foundation, Caldera Foundation, The Curtis and Edith Munson Foundation, The Forrest C. and Frances H. Lattner Foundation, The JPB Foundation, The Kresge Foundation, The Summit Charitable Foundation, Inc., and many other generous organizations and individuals.

The opinions expressed in this book are those of the author(s) and do not necessarily reflect the views of our supporters.

The Freedom of the City

The Freedom of
the City

by
Charles Downing Lay

with introduction and essay by
Thomas J. Campanella

ISLANDPRESS | Washington | Covelo

Publisher's note: *The Freedom of the City,* written by Charles Downing
Lay, was first published in 1926. The introduction and essay by
Thomas J. Campanella were written for this volume in 2022. To
maintain the integrity of Lay's essay, the spelling and grammar have
not been altered. Lay's text is reprinted here largely in its original form,
with the addition of explanatory endnotes by Thomas J. Campanella.

Library of Congress Control Number: 2022946265

All Island Press books are printed on environmentally
responsible materials.

Manufactured in the United States of America
10 9 8 7 6 5 4 3 2 1

Keywords: Battery Park, Central Park, congestion, density, Hudson
Valley, human-scale, the great city, landscape architecture, Long Island,
Marine Park, Robert Moses, New York City, Frederick Law Olmsted,
Olympian, RPAA, Union Square Park, walkable

Contents

Introduction

The Necessity for Congestion

by Thomas J. Campanella

F EW THINGS EXCITE THE PASSIONS MORE THAN A THREAT—real or imagined—to one's home or neighborhood. It is because of such threats that zoning was created. It is because of such threats that density has become such a fraught topic in American cities today. Like guns, density is both devil and redeemer; depending on who you talk to, it's both a cause of suffering and its antidote. For much of our past, we've leaned toward the former. Skepticism about cities in the United States hails back to the founding of the Republic, and has suffused nearly every facet of American society and culture since. Urbanism, and the congestion and overcrowding long associated with it— "the mobs of great cities," as Thomas Jefferson famously put it—were a proxy for all manner of Old-World ills: corruption, crime, moral decay, bondage, and exploitation of the poor. These were all things deemed antithetical to the bright-morning promise of America. Industry and manufacturing, with its insatiable need for labor—cheap, pliant, expendable—should be kept from America's vernal shores. "Let our workshops remain in Europe," Jefferson counseled, lest its exploited minions sully the New World garden with their "manners and principles." The sage of Monticello bet on the farm instead, where the sun-kissed soil would be brought into bounty by proud tillers of the earth. The keys to the kingdom were in calloused hands; for "those who labor in the earth," he avowed, "are the chosen people of God." John Adams concurred: people who lived "chiefly by agriculture, in small numbers, sprinkled over large tracts of land," he wrote, "are not subject to those . . . contagions of madness and folly, which are seen in countries where large numbers live in small places."

Not all of this was idle theory; congestion and density posed some very real hazards. Our first great planned city, Philadelphia, was platted with huge home lots, as "a green country town," wrote William Penn, "which will never be burnt and always be wholesome." Penn witnessed the plague and fire of 1660s London, both of which were greatly accelerated by the city's extreme density. Well into the twentieth century, crowded slums were riven by crime and contagious disease—problems the public-health, park, and infrastructure initiatives of the Reform Era were aimed at fixing.

This antipathy toward the city—and attendant preoccupation with the pastoral—has shape-shifted fluidly with the times. During the Cold War, fear that cities would be targeted by Soviet ICBMs led to proposals to disperse urban populations in the countryside. Futurists like Marshall McLuhan and Alvin Toffler predicted that information technology would make cities obsolete, enabling a "laptopcracy" of knowledge workers to dial in from rural villas. The counterculture of the 1960s yearned to "get back to the garden," launching the Age of Aquarius, not from Central Park but Yasgur's Farm. Even today, magazine and TV advertisements for sport utility vehicles routinely plot an arc away from town and toward the succor and moral clarity of nature—Thoreau's Walden retreat in all-wheel-drive.

Charles Downing Lay certainly appreciated the pleasures of country life, and he wrote eloquently of landscapes and the natural world. He was born and raised in the rural Hudson Valley and spent much of his boyhood—and nearly every summer of adult life—at his family's old home on the Housatonic River. But Lay was an urbanist at heart, a man in love with the city.

The Freedom of the City, long out of print and longer forgotten, is an impassioned rejoinder to American anti-urbanism, a plea for *urbe* from a man equally at home in *rus*. The title was changed from Lay's original, *The Big City*, which his publisher dissuaded him from using. *The Freedom of the City* is a sidelong reference to an old English custom, rooted in the medieval practice of granting liberty to those bound by serfdom, that a city bestows to honor a distinguished citizen or visiting dignitary. Written in a style reminiscent of E. B. Whyte's *Here is New York*, Lay's text is a treatise on the polyvalent delights of city life and—especially—the importance of the singular, essential ingredient that makes it all possible: "congestion." Lay's use of *congestion* differs from its modern, mostly negative meaning, and is closer instead to what we would call *density*. Density, to Lay, is the secret sauce of cities, the singular element that gives London, Paris, or New York its dynamism and magic. He allowed that a city might indeed possess "certain bad habits" or suffer from "high pressure in some of its arteries;" but it was nonetheless "a healthy, growing organism" and not "a cancerous growth to be removed," as many of Lay's professional peers were reasoning at the time.

When Duffield & Company published *The Freedom of the City* in 1926, America's largest metropoles had already begun expanding into their respective hinterlands. This was being driven by the burgeoning popularity of automobiles and the construction of state-of-the-art motorways to run them on. In New York's Westchester and Long Island, an unprecedented network of scenic roads—the Bronx River, Saw Mill, Hutchinson, and Southern State parkways—was spiriting middle-class motorists into the leafy arms of suburbia. An urban exodus was soon under way, one that slowed only with the Great Depression. Elites unsettled by the seemingly endless tide of immigrants flooding the city from Southern and Eastern Europe fled to lily-white Tudor villages—Riverdale, Bronxville, Tuxedo Park, the North Shore of Long Island. Their departure prefigured the more extensive "white flight" of the decades after World War II, a fateful era when ill-conceived federal policy leveled entire urban neighborhoods while underwriting a sprawl of clapboard Monticellos on the edge of town.

Lay saved his sharpest pen for the anti-urbanism in his own profession of city and regional planning. He took special aim at Lewis Mumford and the Regional Planning

Association of America, a brilliant assembly of architects, planners, and housing reformers committed to transplanting the English "Garden City" to America.

Inspired by Patrick Geddes and social visionary Ebenezer Howard, author of *Garden Cities of To-morrow* (1902), the Regionalists considered the hyperdense city to be deeply pathological, something only radical intervention could fix. The populations of big industrial cities, they argued, should be distributed to a constellation of new towns—corseted by greenbelts, linked together by road and rail, with strict land-use controls to prevent them from getting too big or messy. Lay himself had been seduced by this vision earlier in his career. In a 1918 issue of *Landscape Architecture*, he insisted that "our cities must be dispersed instead of concentrated . . . planned in advance for a fixed population per acre," and concluded that "Perhaps the English garden city will be the ideal community, fixing as it does a gratifying mixture of city and country."[1] It is not clear precisely when Lay was struck on this suburban Road to Damascus, but his about-face on dispersal was complete. By the 1920s, Lay was convinced that Howard and his stateside acolytes were misguided dilutionistas with "fear of the city in their hearts," who seemed to take a "morbid delight in . . . the ills of the city" and approached the metropolis like a physician "who sees only sick people and to whom everyone is ill." The idea that a place like New York City—one of humankind's most marvelous creations—could be cashed out for so many tidy greentowns was, to Lay, little more than "an amusing parlor game." Moreover, it ignored a universal truth about cities: density and congestion—the super-concentration of souls in a small space—are not sicknesses to be cured, but an "indispensable condition" of good urbanism. Density and congestion were be celebrated, to be encouraged.

Herein lies the essence of *The Freedom of the City*. Rid a city of its density, eliminate the natural propinquities of a thickly settled place—the incongruous adjacencies, the haphazard minglings and fusions, the *frisson* of people bumping about like frenzied atoms—and you will have lobotomized it. "Congestion is what we came for," Lay writes, "what we stay for, what we hunger for." All the amenities and affordances of a city are "the direct result of its great congestion;" indeed, congestion is "the life of the city. Reduce it below a certain point and much of our ease and convenience disappears."[2]

> We must not rail at the congestion of the city while enjoying its advantages. To say, "wouldn't it be nice if there were fewer people" is to wish it away, or to wish for a special license to enjoy it alone without the annoyance of others having an equal right in the same enjoyment, for it would not exist with fewer people ... If we enjoy the department store with its treasures from all the world, we must realize that it is not there for us alone, that without our million or so neighbors and many guests it could not be there. So it is with all the other things, churches, museums, lectures, music, exhibitions, taxicabs and subways.[3]

Some of the remedies proposed to cure city ills—by Thomas Adams, the RPAA, and others—would have, in fact, made matters worse. One was the insistence that cities be "tempered" by nature, that a panoply of urban troubles would be cured if the city would just suck down a big

green smoothie. Lay allowed that a "hint of country pleasures" was helpful; only a fool would object to a Central or
Prospect Park. But these, he argued, cannot be allowed "to
interfere with the essential quality of the city" by flooding
it with too much open space. "We should get over our fear
of the city, cease trying to ameliorate it by giving it weak
echoes of the country or by making it innocuous by great
dilution, but try rather to make this new machine a good
one that will work." Moreover, the natural world was never
fully absent in even the densest urban centers. "Is the city
any further from Nature than the country?" After all, "the
same wind blows in from the open sea whether we be at
the Battery or at Montauk Point . . . the sun shines on city
as on country, and moon and stars are the same."[4] Not
one to let a snub go unpunished, a sour Mumford savaged
Lay's book in the *New Republic*. Lay was a "good megalo-
politan," he sneered, who "looks forward with buoyant hope
not merely to higher cities, but to a continuous expanse of
them over all the available countryside." To Mumford, neither *Freedom* nor its pro-rural companion counterpart by
Walter Prichard Eaton, *A Bucolic Attitude* (discussed later),
were worth reading; the ideas within were "negligible."[5]

The great Manhattan grid—projected on the rural
island in 1811 and later extended to much of New York
City—was another element Lay considered essential to
Gotham's verve and vitality. "The plan of New York City,"
wrote one reviewer, "fascinates Mr. Lay like a lover."[6] Here,
too, Lay's opinion was in the minority among architects
and city planners of the time. "It is customary to make fun
of New York's plan," he writes, "and it has indeed some unfortunate details, but on the whole, it fits our needs better
than many others."

One wonders sometimes if the secret of our great growth is not partly in a plan perfectly adapted to congestion, which produces so much in convenience at a comparatively low cost in money? It is the fact of dividing the costs of streets, with all their service of sewer, water, gas, electricity and unequalled rapid transit among so many people that makes the big city possible.[7]

∼

How relevant is *The Freedom of the City* today? Does its message about the necessity for congestion still hold, given that the problems confronting our cities are so much more complex than in the Jazz Age? Can its author possibly speak to our vexed times—of lightspeed communication and social media mobs; of yawning wealth gaps and surging global migration; of urgent calls for racial justice and looming chaos of climate change? This is a book, after all, written nearly a century ago by a very dead, very white, very male author. Several academics consulted on this project pointed out as much, that we have heard enough from heteropatriarchal WASPs like Lay; in effect, that Lay should be silenced because of his race, class, and gender— itself an example of intolerance. Lay was not robber-baron rich, but he was a fortunate son who enjoyed a bountiful life—Ivy-League-educated, well-married, shuttling between a historic townhouse in Brooklyn Heights and the summer shade of ancestral elms. He was able to escape the grit and din of New York whenever he wished. The lens through which Lay studied the urban scene was a highly privileged one. The conditions he celebrates, of density and congestion, were sources of grinding misery for those on society's margins—a fact he glosses over or completely ignores. Lay's New York is not the Lower East Side of the peasant Italian or the threadbare tenements of Black Harlem. Did he understand what density meant to the Alabama sharecropper huddled in a cold-water flat? The Jew from the Pale of Settlement working 14-hour days in a crowded sweatshop? Nor does Lay have anything much to say about the vast outer borough neighborhoods in Brooklyn and Queens then under construction, a paradise of sorts for children of the very immigrants whom Jacob Riis documented—who yearned for anything *but* the density, congestion, and chaos of the city. As a review in the *Christian Science Monitor* put it, "Lay's vaulting enthusiasm is of the high-pressure type that ignores many of the loose ends of his urban philosophy."[8]

Perhaps the most egregious of these "loose ends" is Lay's insistence that the millions of people in New York were all there by choice; "None are held in slavery," he asserts, "except to their own desires, and none would leave if given the opportunity."[9] This, of course, is a colossal overstatement, astonishingly blind to the misery and privation that was city life for countless citizens on class-and-caste rungs lower than Lay's. Professionally, at least, Lay was well aware of the plight of those who had little choice but to suffer the density and congestion of the inner city. Shortly after World War II, he began working on plans for the rehabilitation of East Harlem, then rapidly becoming one of the city's most blighted neighborhoods. Of course, New York was no longer the place it had been when Lay wrote *Freedom*; the city's population jumped by more than two million between 1920 and 1950 while, in East Harlem, a surge of impoverished immigrants from Puerto Rico turned what was already a crowded district into a boiling cauldron. Congestion, alas, might not have been the universal good Lay had once argued. "There seems no question about the increasing cost and discomfort of city living," he wrote in a letter to Rita Morgan of the East Harlem Council for Community Planning, "which has reached such a point that its innumerable advantages . . . are unattainable by many people." The aim of Lay's Harlem plan was "to reduce the density of Manhattans [*sic*] population per acre; to bring about . . . a more evenly spread population in order to reduce the pressure on transportation, the congestion of street traffic and to equalize real values throughout the Island."[10]

And yet, for all his blind spots, Lay's core argument remains solid. *The Freedom of the City* was prescient in 1926 and is timely now. Certainly, the essentials of good urbanism extolled in the book—human scale, diversity, walkability, the serendipities of the street; above all, density—are articles of faith among architects and urbanists today. They were charged with fresh meaning in 1961 with publication of Jane Jacobs's *Death and Life of Great American Cities*, a celebration of traditional city form that almost single-handedly stopped the postwar urban renewal juggernaut. At the very nadir of America's urban arc in the mid-1970s, Rem Koolhaas's *Delirious New York*—a "retroactive manifesto" for Manhattan—echoed Lay's focus on congestion as the lodestone of urbanism. To Koolhaas, New York is the purest expression of the urban idea, where the alchemy of real-estate economics and building technology plays out on a neutral chessboard, a gridded spaceframe wholly indifferent "to topography, to what exists." While its basic unit—the standard city block—is restrictive in terms of x-y field, it permits, even begs, almost infinite expression in the vertical dimension (the z axis). "Manhattan represents the apotheosis of the ideal of density per se, both of population and of infrastructure," writes Koolhaas. "Its architecture promotes a state of congestion on all possible levels, and exploits this congestion to inspire and support . . . a unique *culture of congestion*."[11]

But we stand at a curious threshold today, one that makes Lay's paean to urban density more vital than ever. Density and congestion are under siege, especially in our most productive and thriving cities. That we face this conundrum is itself ironic, and calls to mind the maxim "Be careful what you wish for." In recent decades, that old American antipathy to the city has given way to a new rage for life at the metropolitan core. As the urban crime wave of the '70s and '80s ebbed (the reasons why are still debated and controversial), middle-class professionals began returning to the city, often to the same places—Park Slope, the Upper West Side, Boston's South End—abandoned for suburbia by earlier generations. They were drawn by the same qualities of urbanism that Lay and Jacobs had praised: the serendipity of crowds, the wide array of cultural amenities, the diversity of peoples, life thick and throbbing with possibility—a concentrate of humanity itself. But this "rediscovery" of the urban—by a well-educated, largely white demographic—is not without complications. However hardscrabble New York's old neighborhoods may have been by the 1970s, they were not void of people. White flight had created a vacuum that was promptly filled—by Puerto Ricans, Blacks from the rural South and, after 1965, immigrants from Asia, the West Indies, and Latin America. These poor, often impoverished newcomers—renters especially—were edged out by a tide of gentrification. Gracious old neighborhoods in Brownstone Brooklyn or the West Village became, over time, new bastions of wealth. Family-run stores and gritty supermarkets were replaced by bistros and boutiques.

As rents continued to escalate, the gentrificants themselves began to fear being priced out of home and 'hood. By the early 2000s, the pro-development "growth machine" that had long set the planning agenda in our most vibrant cities was running into increasingly stiff resistance, with opposition to proposed projects—even urbanistically good projects—driven mostly by "renters who fear that the development will make their homes less affordable, and either cause them to . . . leave the neighborhood or change the neighborhood to something less familiar and appealing to them."[12] Density—that essential stuff of good urbanism—was suddenly the enemy. The NIMBY (Not In My Back Yard) phenomenon, long associated with conservative, white suburbia and its "mercenary concern with property values" had begun to rear its head in America's most liberal cities. Given the paucity of yards in places like Manhattan, a more appropriate term—the one I'll use hence—might be NADA: No Additional Density Allowed.[13]

In a 2018 study published in the *Journal of Land Use*, Vicki Been traced such resistance to several factors. For one, Americans were moving less than at any time since

1950—even within counties and cities. Putting down roots, as either a renter or homeowner, magnifies one's level of political engagement and her longing to protect a community from change. Proposals seen as threatening one's living costs, quality of life, or status quo are thus vehemently opposed. In time, NADA opposition becomes codified in a series of measures meant to slow or stall development. The result has been a drastic throttling of residential development in the very places people want to be: big, booming, productive cities where the highest-paying, most-promising jobs are; where the commute times are shortest; where the social opportunities are richest and the amenity bench is deepest.[14] In New York, Boston, San Francisco, and other high-value cities, municipalities have "adopted land use practices," writes Been, "long associated with suburbs— imposing more restrictions on land through downzonings, charging significant fees for development approval, and taking land off the market through programs to preserve historic landmarks and open space."[15] Getting something built in these places is like navigating Kafka's castle blind-folded. "The permitting process in Manhattan," writes Edward Glaeser, "is an arduous, unpredictable, multiyear odyssey involving a dizzying array of regulations, environmental and otherwise, and a host of agencies"—topped off by a typically bruising encounter with "neighborhood activists and historical preservationists."[16]

Why is this such a problem? A city is a supercomputer, an urban information processor that "turns the interactions of a market economy and its social networks into a mechanism of human ingenuity," writes Ryan Avent. Cities are "an informational infrastructure in and of themselves," he

stresses, "amplifying the human capital of the workers employed there and fueling the development of the new ideas
that are the bedrock of prosperity." Density and congestion
enable these interactions, make the urban mainframe do
its magic. Supercomputer pioneer Seymour Cray understood this when he bent the chassis of his famous Cray-1
into a cylinder, to shorten the distance signals had to travel
between components. Doing so effectively densified the
machine's circuitry, reducing cycle times and dramatically
boosting processing speeds. The Cray-1 was an order of
magnitude faster than earlier supercomputers, which ar-
rayed processors on broad, flat panels—suburban circuitry,
if you will. A city is a suburb folded, like a sheet of paper,
into a compact square. Density "is what cities do," Avent
asserts, echoing Lay, "and what we want them to do."

Fettering a city's density is akin to unfolding Cray's
supercomputer, slowing it down and yet expecting it to
function as fast and as splendidly as before. "Our thriving
cities fall short of their potential because we constantly
rein them in," writes Avent, "and we rein them in because
we worry that urban growth will be unpleasant." Zoning
out residential development in the face of surging demand
makes a scarce commodity scarcer still, driving housing
costs through the proverbial roof. NADA residents fear
change and pull up the drawbridge, effectively barring new
workers from moving there and stifling the urban economy—and the nation's productivity—in the process. "By
severely limiting new housing production," writes Nolan
Gray, "we have made moving to our most prosperous regions a dubious proposition. Your income might double
if you were to move from Orlando to San Francisco, but

your housing costs would quadruple."[17] As a result, coveted places like Manhattan, San Francisco, and Brownstone Brooklyn are gradually becoming playgrounds of rich, increasingly inaccessible to the very sort of hungry, rising strivers who have long charged our cities with passion and energy.

This is helping drive the loathsome wedge of income inequality ever deeper into society's hide. Property values lofted by zoning-induced scarcity keep low-wealth service workers from being able to afford housing in places where the good jobs are, impeding their own climb up the economic ladder. At the same time, these restrictions enable existing homeowners—an already privileged group—to capture rising real estate values at the expense of renters, "adding further to their wealth while limiting the ability of others to build wealth through homeownership ,"writes Been.[18] Needless to say, this has had a disproportionate impact on communities of color. A number of recent studies point to a positive relationship between NADA restrictions and racial segregation, and between density limits generally and smaller Black and Latino populations. As Jonathan T. Rothwell of the Brookings Institution has found, anti-density zoning regulations "curtail the exit of minority groups from segregated communities by limiting the supply of affordable housing in integrated areas."[19]

~

If *The Freedom of the City* was so prescient a book, why has it not become a widely read classic? The likely answer is that Lay had a series of unfortunate clashes with his publisher, Duffield & Company, at a time when the firm was on rocky financial ground. The trouble began when the Duffield executive who signed Lay's book, Frederick Hoppin, informed the author that he was resigning as president. Orphaned, Lay's manuscript was assigned to a junior editor, Horace Green, who already had a full load of books he was marshalling toward publication. *Freedom* was put at the end of the queue. Lay was also informed that Green had "some new ideas" about the book—words no author likes to hear. In a letter written just before Thanksgiving 1925, Green asked Lay if he might "perhaps work in something about city gardens for various pocketbooks—flower pots on the balcony, the charm of serving coffee in the back yard . . . that sort of thing?" Hoping to stage a stirring country–city duel of sorts, Green proposed having Lay's treatise "answered by some author pledged to the rural side of the argument," suggesting that his pro-urban argument be offset by "such spirits as O. Henry who were barren of ideas in the country and must be surrounded by walls and steam heaters." Lay was not amused, to put it mildly, and fired back a terse note that promised nothing.[20]

By February 1926, Lay's book was clearly languishing in publication limbo. It is not known why Hoppin left Duffield, but the firm began having serious management problems around the time of his resignation; at the time, Green himself admitted to Lay that the press "had done no selling for three or four months." For reasons unclear, Lay had already threatened Duffield with legal action for defamation of character. With Green's shocking revelation about book sales, he now demanded to be released from his contract. Though Lay was talked out of this, he and the publisher continued to clash—over manuscript length, publication schedule, unapproved changes to the text, and a failure to get Lay the galleys in time for him to make corrections. None of this boded well for a successful book launch. *The Freedom of the City* was finally published in June 1926, paired with the promised rustic rebuttal—*A Bucolic Attitude* by Walter Prichard Eaton. The books were reviewed together by Henry James Forman in the *New York Times*. Forman begrudgingly lauded Lay for his prose, which "rises at times and in (small) spots, to lyrical altitudes that remind one of Whitman." Most others also appraised the books as a pair, with Eaton's generally garnering more favorable treatment. A New York theater critic and Yale professor who retired to the Berkshires, Eaton was a more talented writer than Lay; but the timing of the books' release, the summer solstice, mightily favored Eaton's subject. The density and congestion of New York City is least palatable in summer, especially in an age before air conditioning—with insufferable heat and windows opened to all the clang and clatter of urban life. Had the books been released in the weeks before Christmas, for example, with the city alight with lights and joy and rural New England dreary and snowbound, perhaps things would have turned in Lay's favor. In any case, while Eaton's book is readily available today on antiquarian book sites, printed copies of *Freedom* are almost impossible to find—suggesting that Duffield may have purposely underprinted the title, done little or nothing to promote it, or even pulled it after publication. Did Lay's publisher let his book slip beneath the waves as punishment for the author's recalcitrance? We will likely never know.[21]

Charles D. Lay in 1926. (Carl A. Kroch Library, Cornell University)

The Life
and Work of
Charles Downing Lay

by Thomas J. Campanella

*T*HE FINE ARTS DO NOT IMMEDIATELY jump to mind when one thinks of the Olympic Games, but until the 1940s, "Art" was an official category of competition. It was catholic in scope, with subsections that included architecture, painting and graphics, sculpture, music, and literature (lyric, dramatic, or epic). Architecture included both building design and "Designs for Town Planning." Naturally, athletics had to be the focus of any submitted work: "Only those designs will be admitted having as object the practice of sport." It was in this manner that the bookish, bespectacled Charles Downing Lay became an Olympian, awarded a silver medal in town planning at the infamous 1936 Olympic summer games in Berlin. Opened by Hitler and poisoned by Nazi propaganda, it was the first televised, radio-broadcast Olympiad, captured in an epic documentary by Leni Riefenstahl. Predictably enough, the

Germans dominated the games, taking five gold, five silver, and two bronze medals in the art section alone. The Americans won 56 medals at the games, the very first of which was Lay's silver. He won for a masterplan to design an immense waterfront park in Brooklyn—a vast playscape of gamesmanship and competitive sport that, some speculated, might itself host a future Olympiad. Though a trifling achievement next to Jessie Owens's four-gold triumph in track and field, Lay's unlikely opening medal made news throughout the United States.[1]

Charles Downing Lay was a Hudson Valley boy who came to the city and fell in love. To him, New York was humanity distilled, a teeming crucible of civilization itself. But Lay had Emersonian range in his topophilia. He was that rare urbanist who savored nature and studied the rural landscape, who—to paraphrase Emerson—could appreciate a fine barn as well as a good tragedy. Lay's life's work was a studied disavowal of that depleted American binary of country and city, a virtuosity that enabled him to write with equal eloquence about canoes and subways, saltmarshes, wild rice, camping, or bus terminals. He was born in the Newburgh on September 3, 1877. His father, Oliver Ingraham Lay, was a prominent New York artist who had studied painting with Thomas Hicks and whose portraiture included prominent figures of the time—among them Ulysses S. Grant and the Shakespearean actor Edwin Booth, brother of Lincoln's assassin. Lay's grandparents, George Cowles Lay and Julia Anna Hartness, had come to the city from Connecticut in 1837, residing first at 6 Allen Street in the 10th Ward, where Oliver was born, and moving later to 128 East 24th Street—a place Charles would have known

Charles D. Lay's second-prize certificate of honor, Organizing Committee of the XI Olympiad, Berlin, 1936. (Carl A. Kroch Library, Cornell University)

as a child. Lay's mother was Hester Marian Wait, whose sister Mary married pomologist Charles Downing—Lay's namesake and brother of the pioneering horticulturalist and landscape gardener Andrew Jackson Downing.

While his father's family endowed Charles with a life-long love of art, it was the Downing side that led him to landscape architecture, to which he arrived in a round-about way. Lay attended J. H. Morse's English, Classical, and Mathematical School for Boys on West 38th Street in New York—which professed "to prepare boys thoroughly for the best colleges and scientific schools"—and continued on to the School of Architecture at Columbia University in 1896. Unhappy with the school's traditional Beaux Arts curriculum—and doing poorly as a result—Lay

Oliver Ingraham Lay, Portrait of a Baby [Charles D. Lay at two years old], 1879, oil on canvas. (Private collection)

looked into a new course of study in landscape architecture at Harvard. Established in 1900 by Frederick Law Olmsted, Jr., son of the great park planner, Harvard's program was the first in the nation to offer a formal degree in landscape architecture. Lay completed his studies there in 1902, graduating with a B.S. in Arte Topiaria—only the second student to do so. Shortly thereafter, he took a job with Daniel W. Langton, a charter member of the

Charles D. Lay at Columbia, c1900 (detail). (Carl A. Kroch Library, Cornell University)

American Society of Landscape Architects whose Fifth Avenue practice focused on private commissions in New York and New Jersey. Because Langton was a consultant to the Hudson County Park Commission, the job introduced Lay to public work as well. The largest project in the office at the time was Lincoln Park in Jersey City.[2]

Lay remained with Langton until 1904, when he opened an office of his own. In the same year, he also took up studies at the Art Students League; his teachers included Mahonri Young, Gifford Beal and Allen Tucker (who later edited the catalog for the 1913 Armory show).[3] Lay became a skilled painter, watercolorist, and printmaker. He exhibited etchings and watercolors at the Weyhe and Kraushaar galleries with Edward Hopper, Maurice Prendergast, and

Alexander Calder; his work was acquired by the Whitney, Brooklyn Museum, and Metropolitan Museum of Art. In October 1904, Lay married a Brooklyn girl named Laura Braithwaite Gill, whose family lived at 19 Montgomery Place. Laura's father, Thomas L. Gill, was born in Barbados and emigrated to the United States in 1869, where he made a fortune in the lumber trade. The couple lived with Laura's family for several years before purchasing a home at 11 Cranberry Street in Brooklyn Heights. They would reside there for the next 50 years, spending summers at Lay's paternal home in Connecticut. Laura was active in Brooklyn society and helped organize the Brooklyn Woman Suffrage Association. She cultivated a keen interest in the design arts, creating a playground for the Brooklyn Friends School and often joining Charles at his office to develop planting plans. In both the 1925 New York State census and 1940 federal census, she reported her occupation as "landscape architect."[4]

In 1906, Lay began collaborating with a former classmate, Henry Vincent Hubbard, who had graduated just ahead of him at Harvard and was now teaching there. The men found plentiful work designing formal gardens for well-heeled clients in New York and New England, and in 1910 took on a third partner—Robert Wheelwright of Boston. Lay and Wheelwright had already discussed launching a new quarterly for the American Society of Landscape Architects, and later invited Hubbard to join in founding *Landscape Architecture* magazine. The "Landscapers Three," as they called themselves, would edit the publication together for the next decade. Lay was a prolific writer and editor, contributing scores of articles, essays, and opinion pieces over the years—not only to the journal he helped found, but to a gamut of newspapers and popular magazines.[5] Lay's public service career began in August 1911, when the New York City Park Board appointed him landscape architect. He succeeded the aging Samuel B. Parsons, Jr.—a former partner of Olmsted and Vaux whose family nursery had accidentally introduced the chestnut blight to America. Lay's tenure as the city's chief landscape architect began auspiciously enough: when Lay's name was brought forward at a meeting of the Park Board at the Arsenal, the lions in the nearby Central Park Menagerie roared in seeming approval. But the job was fraught. Lay had the misfortune to serve under Charles Bunstein Stover, the most eccentric park commissioner in city history. Appointed by Mayor William Gaynor in 1910, Stover gained immediate notoriety for a series of baffling disappearances. He vanished for six weeks shortly before taking office, ostensibly to immerse himself in a study of Italian gardens. When three lion cubs were born at the Menagerie, Stover dropped out again for weeks, supposedly to come up with names for the baby cats. A final vanishing act in October 1913 so alarmed city officials that footage of Stover was patched together by Pathé Frères and shown in movie halls all across America. However colorful, such antics did not bode well for an agency in desperate need of leadership.

Indeed, Lay found the parks department—not to mention the parks themselves—in a state of almost total chaos. Central Park was in especially bad shape—lawns littered and balding, slopes eroded, trees vandalized, soils compacted. "Any owner of a small place, even though he had

Charles D. Lay, etching of a tree, nd. (Carl A. Kroch Library, Cornell University)

Charles D. Lay, The Concert, nd. (Carl A. Kroch Library, Cornell University)

no interest in gardening or trees," Lay complained, "would be distressed if his backyard were in a condition approaching that of Central Park." The elms along the park on Fifth Avenue, diseased and misshapen from years of ignorant pruning, "would be a disgrace to any city." Worse yet, the department was woefully understaffed. There were few draftsmen available, and most parks lacked even the most basic survey or topographic maps. Lay was forced to use Central Park visitor guides to specify plantings around The Pond and Gapstow Bridge. Predictably, he clashed from the start with both Stover and Mayor Gaynor. Lay could be obstinate and was often politically reckless—especially when dealing with figures of authority. Throughout his career, he alienated powerful individuals—most fatally Robert Moses, as we will see—rather than compromise on even minor issues. Lay was a deeply principled man who refused to forgo his values for political expedience—a costly habit in a rough and tumble place like New York.[6]

Lay's initial clash with Stover was over a bowling lawn and running track in Battery Park that Mayor Gaynor had personally requested. He turned down the request, for one of Lay's most inflexible rules was the total separation of park and playground facilities. "Parks and playgrounds are like east and west and can never meet," he explained. Lay also insisted that he approve all park plans before they were sent to the Municipal Art Commission for review. Stover refused this and blocked the release of Lay's first annual report as punishment. The men clashed again over an ill-advised series of fenced play spaces in the median of upper Seventh Avenue. Stover cheered these as "the longest playground in the country;" to Lay, they were sun-baked cages bathed in automobile exhaust. Things got more heated still when, in June 1912, Lay vetoed Stover's impulsive scheme to demolish the historic Arsenal—then, as now, headquarters of the Parks Department—to clear the site for the old Lenox Library on Fifth Avenue, which Henry Clay Frick had offered to the city on the condition it be moved.[7] Gaynor's original directive to the Park Board was to hire a landscape architect of a "subordinate frame of mind." As Lay tersely put it, "I am not built that way." Few were surprised when he resigned on May 1, 1913, explaining that his professional reputation would suffer if he continued in a position so handicapped by a lack of staff and even maps. "I believe the position of Landscape Architect is an important one," he wrote to the Park Board, but whoever filled it next would need "sufficient help to prepare thoroughly studied plans in advance of their need."[8]

Despite the brevity of his tenure as city landscape architect, Lay left a mark on his town. His layout of Union Square Park, a collaboration with architect Thomas Hastings, brings pleasure to countless New Yorkers to this day. He upgraded Battery Park, designed a playground for John Jay Park, drafted a plan for Bryant Park, modernized the old pond at Linden Park in Corona (Park of the Americas today), nearly succeeded in removing the Tweed Courthouse and the bloated old Post Office building to expand City Hall Park, and completed a plan for Forest Park in Queens just days before stepping down. Lay was also responsible for planting hundreds of cherry trees gifted by the Japanese government for the 1909 Hudson-Fulton Celebration. The first shipment of 2,100 saplings was said to have been lost at sea but was, in fact, quietly destroyed by a Department of Agriculture still reeling from the chestnut blight catastrophe. (The cherry trees were found to be crawling with "strange insects" that were feared might vector a ruinous disease.) A second shipment arrived in 1912, and the trees were planted at Grant's Tomb and Claremont Park. The final specimens were set in the ground that April, in a ceremony attended by 5,000 people. Following speeches and selections from The Mikado and American Fantasia, 13 kimono-clad girls carrying tiny spades proceeded to plant their cherry whips. Commissioner Stover that day renamed the park *Sakura*—cherry blossom in Japanese—the name it still bears today.[9]

After his embattled turn as Gotham's chief park designer, Lay retreated to the relative peace of solo practice, designing estates for a long list of well-heeled clients. This was an age of great fortunes as yet unencumbered by an income tax, which created plentiful work for the landscape architecture profession. Between 1900 and the Great Depression, the field had largely abandoned the public-works ethos of its founders to become something of a court profession to America's über-rich. As a Harvard man, Lay was anomalous in pursuing such "country place" commissions. His alma mater was long associated with the Anglo-romantic park tradition of the Olmsteds—what Lay called the English school, which he criticized as a praxis that "assumes only to copy the accidents of a partly tamed nature."[10] It was Cornell, rather (and ironically, given its agricultural-school roots)—Harvard's great rival in the early years of American landscape architectural education—that focused almost exclusively on country-place

Formal garden at Marble House, Dorset, Vermont (Manley-Lefèvre House) (Photo by Pamela Polston, Seven Days Vermont, 2014)

formalism, training practitioners in the traditions of Italian Renaissance villa and garden design. Indeed, despite studying under his son, Lay had little praise for Frederick Law Olmsted, revered father of the field. He bemoaned the "deification of Olmsted" and blamed a "reverential attitude to his work" for stultifying the profession. "Central Park was a brilliant idea," he wrote to Wheelwright, "carried out by a person of no great artistic capacity."[11]

Lay marketed himself to clients as an "artistically trained garden expert" whose skills could "improve or refine a garden or a country place in order to bring about a higher organization and make it a true expression of the owner's personality." There was no shortage of work in this era of surging economic growth. He laid out the C. W.

Power and L. W. Dodge estates in Pittsfield, Massachusetts and the J. Percy Bartram estate on Caritas Island in
Stamford, Connecticut. He created a bosquet and garden
pool for Charlton Yarnall in Newtown Square, Pennsylvania and planned the grounds of the S. Forry Laucks estate
in Wrightsville, Pennsylvania—with terraces, loggia, bath-
houses, and a lily pond perched high above the Susque-
hanna River. Perhaps his most accomplished garden was
executed for the journalist, diplomat, and business writer
Edwin Lefèvre of Dorset, Vermont. The Lefèvre house
was built in 1820 of locally quarried marble, and Lay used
the same stone for its pergola, water steps and fountains,
tea house, pool, walls, and planters carved with animals
and ships. He placed a pair of fountains on either side of
the Italianate garden's central axis, each bearing a Latin
inscription. One, from Ovid's *Letters from the Black Sea*,
could well have described the designer's stoical nature:
gutta cavat lapidem non vi sed saepe cadendo (a water drop
hollows a stone not by force, but by falling often). The
Lefèvre estate is now home to the Marble House Project,
which offers residential fellowships to artists, writers, and
musicians.

However lucrative, these country place commissions
never fully quelled Lay's interest in public works. He
collaborated with Arnold Brunner on a general plan for
Albany, which proposed an ambitious extension of the
capital city's system of parks and parkways. He planned a
civic center for Verona, New Jersey and laid out the cam-
pus for the New York State Normal and Training School
at Cortland (SUNY Cortland today). And he often found
himself back on familiar city turf. He drafted a restoration

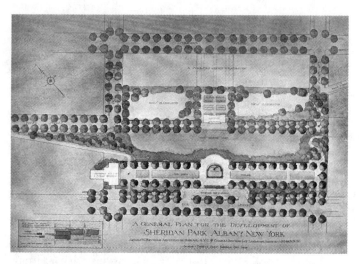

Charles D. Lay and Gilmore D. Clarke, A General Plan for the Development of Sheridan Park. (From Charles D. Lay and Arnold W. Brunner, Studies for Albany, 1914)

plan for Madison Square Park and its historic English elms, and prepared designs for several gardens and monuments in Central Park—including an elaborate war memorial by Carrère and Hastings; a memorial dedicated to "Boy Mayor" John Purroy Mitchel, who died in a freak Army Air Service flight-training accident in 1918; and a Children's Garden in honor of Frances Hodgson Burnett, author of *Little Lord Fauntleroy*, for a site just west of the Conservatory Water (what ultimately became the Hans Christian Anderson Memorial).[12]

During the first World War, Lay served with the U. S. Department of Labor's Bureau of Industrial Housing and Transportation, laying out subdivisions for defense workers in Butler and Erie, Pennsylvania. In the 1920s, he laid out the grounds of the National Academy of Sciences in

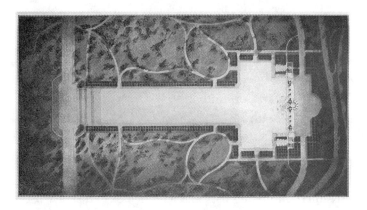

Charles D. Lay and Thomas Hastings, plan view of proposed World War I memorial for Central Park. (From The War Memorial for the City of New York, 1923. Carl A. Kroch Library, Cornell University.)

Charles D. Lay and Thomas Hastings, perspective view of proposed World War I memorial for Central Park. (From The War Memorial for the City of New York, 1923. Carl A. Kroch Library, Cornell University.)

Washington and collaborated with Hjalmar E. Skougor and James Gamble Rogers II to plan Arvida, a model town for the Aluminum Company of America in northern Quebec. This was followed by a commission from the Nassau County Committee—one that put him on a collision course with Robert Moses. Lay's client wanted him to plan a park system for Long Island that countered the one Moses had drafted as head of the Long Island State Park Commission. This was one of eleven regional commissions comprising the State Council of Parks, proposed by Moses in his 1922 State Park Plan for New York and funded by a bond issue passed by the legislature in 1924. Moses lost no time condemning land for his parks and parkways, but he ran into a hailstorm of organized opposition from wealthy landowners in Wheatley Hills whose vast estates he threatened to pierce with the Northern State Parkway. It was this faction that hired Lay to come up with an alternative.

Like a true professional, Lay went to bat for his client. He accused Moses of pushing plans forward with "excessive haste" and "squandering the State's money on ill-considered projects, which when consummated are found to be inadequate or useless." Lay reproached the Long Island State Park Commission for a lack of transparency; a public works program of such immense scale and expense "should be a matter of discussion," he argued, "of seeking all the advice possible, of calm deliberation, and of orderly and continuous action.

The planning and the scheming must first be done in detail in order that everything may be anticipated and

arranged for. Nothing unforeseen must arise. It is important, too, to take the public into one's confidence and to
secure popular support and cooperation. To arouse antag-
onism and obstruction at the beginning may jeopardize
the whole plan and make it impossible to carry through in
full . . . Whatever the Long Island Commission does will
be extremely hard to undo and it will effect the growth,
the prosperity and the social life of all Long Island for
generations to come."[13]

As his Wheatley Hills clients hoped, Lay recommended that "the whole territory of the northerly part of
Nassau County be omitted from any plans for parks or
parkways," and that the proposed Northern Parkway be
rerouted as a "Middle Island Highway." Lay's proposed
alternative route would follow an alignment from Queens
south around Lake Success, down Marcus Avenue toward
Hillside Manor, and on to East Williston, Carle Place,
and Westbury. "From there," he explained, "the road could
run on a new line passing north of Hicksville to Plainview,
Melville, and on southward to Lake Ronkonkoma"—an
alignment almost precisely that of the Long Island Ex-
pressway today. Lay seemed to take naturally to clients
of wealth and privilege. This was partly due to his own
upbringing, but also conditioned by his long association
with country-place clients. His defense of the Wheatley
Hills crowd was not the first time he had sided with elites;
while serving with New York City, he nixed a proposal to
open the sloping gardens behind Columbia Heights to the
public—a move that would have granted the public access
to the bluff above New York harbor decades before Robert

Moses built the Brooklyn Heights Promenade. Lay argued that creating a park here (his own neighborhood, not insignificantly) would not only be "a nuisance to the property owners," but also "increase immorality, and . . . be in every way objectionable."[14]

Lay's Nassau County plan not only censured the route of the Northern State Parkway, but the very idea of the modern parkway itself. The first of these motor roads was built in Westchester in the early 1920s by an extraordinary team of designers—many of whom, such as landscape architect Gilmore D. Clarke, Moses would later recruit to New York City. Moses made no secret of wanting to extend to Long Island the "Westchester model" of parkways used to link up a regional matrix of parks and recreation spaces. To Lay, there was little difference between the modern motor parkway and earlier uses of the term, specifically Eastern and Ocean parkways in Brooklyn, which Olmsted lifted whole cloth from Haussmann's Paris. "The parkway idea," Lay resolved, "belongs with the driving horse in the past." To him, the roads were "essentially a high brow invention to protect the delicate sensibilities of the wealthy from the offenses of manufacturing, of trade and of adjoining property owners."[15] Motorists, he argued—with no proof—had no interest in viewing pastoral scenery along their roads, but only wanted to reach their destination as soon as possible. "The chief delight of motoring," Lay offered, "is the complete change of scene which it makes possible."

We would like to leave our homes in the city and without delay or interest in the familiar things of the first forty miles, be in an entirely different environment, where we

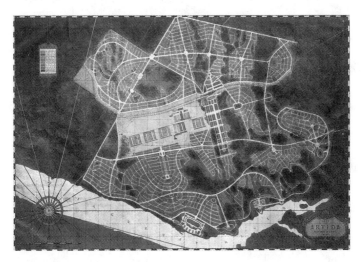

Master plan for Arvida, Quebec, c1926. (Courtesy Centre d'Histoire Arvida)

could ride slowly on unfamiliar roads or park the car and get out to picnic or camp, or rest under a tree or throw pebbles in the water. How to get there matters little so that it be quickly.[16]

Whether or not Lay was correct in assuming that "since the motorist has usually an objective . . . the beauty of the scenery on the way is of comparatively little interest to him" is debatable. Certainly, such a hurried attitude would become commonplace after World War II, when the parkway ideal was largely set aside in favor of high-speed expressways. Certainly, Lay's position on parkways did little to endear him to Moses, a man whose "cherished ambition" was to use just the sort of infrastructure Lay panned "to weave together the loose strands and frayed edges of New York's arterial and metropolitan tapestry."[17]

Oddly, Lay himself changed his tune on the subject after the war, when he launched a campaign to build a parkway along the Housatonic River. He envisioned this road as anything but solely a means of getting from urban point A to rural point B "without delay." "The attraction of this country," he wrote of the Housatonic valley, "is its primitive, unspoiled condition. Much of it is inaccessible, and this is the great reason for urging the building of a scenic parkway." Doing so, he argued—oblivious to the perils therein—"will open it all to settlement and, by means of short connections to new parks along the river, give easy access to all the delights of the river in scenery, sports and recreation."[18] The road was to run north from the sound on both sides of the river, connect to the Merritt Parkway and continue on for some 75 miles "through wooded hill country to the Massachusetts line at North Canaan."[19] Akin to the Bronx River and other early parkways in Westchester, Lay imagined the Housatonic Parkway as a conservation play, an effort "to preserve and enhance the natural beauties of the river," he explained, "and to prevent its being ruined by eager promoters who are even now beginning their hasty subdivisions."[20] A bill introduced to the Connecticut General Assembly in January 1945 failed to pass, as did a second one in 1947. Lay nimbly changed his strategy, founding the Housatonic Valley Association the very next year—today one of the oldest and most accomplished environmental advocacy groups in New England.

The Northern State Parkway aside, Lay seems to have had a special gift for antagonizing Robert Moses. He did so again by pushing the idea of a Metropolitan Planning

Commission to coordinate regional development matters between the urbanized eastern end of Long Island and sub-urban–rural Nassau and Suffolk counties—another idea hatched in the course of his work for the Nassau County Committee. This thoroughly sane idea was something he had previously discussed with Moses, who flatly rejected it. Not only was such a commission unnecessary, railed Moses, but agitating for its approval "would be positively harmful to the efforts now under way for park planning in the metropolitan district." And as if this was not enough, Lay then seeded opposition to a state park at Jones Beach, the very place Moses wanted for the crown jewel of his Long Island parks. The Nassau County Committee had no objections to a great ocean playground at Jones Beach, which Lay himself had recommended. But it wanted this park to be managed locally—not by the state but by a body modeled, as Lay counseled, on the highly success-ful Westchester County Park Commission.[21] Lay couldn't have known it at the time, but this work for the Nassau County Committee would prove costly to his career. In the 1920s, Robert Moses was still a Robin Hood figure of sorts, a crusader for the people whom even the *New York Times* championed as "a great and good man." Thwart-ing his plans on behalf of the Gatsby crowd earned Lay the enmity of a man who had an elephant memory and a penchant for revenge, who almost singlehandedly ruled the public works arena in New York for the next forty years. There is no telling how much greater Lay's influence might have been had he not indelibly etched his name into the Mosaic book of enemies. This became evident

*Aerial view looking south over Marine Park and Gerritsen Creek, ca.
1931; lighter areas are fresh sand pumped as fill from Rockaway inlet.
(Photo by Fairchild Aerial Survey, Inc. Collection of the author)*

a decade later in Brooklyn, when Moses—now commissioner of the unified city parks department—snatched
from Lay what might have been his greatest work.

Gerritsen Creek, an inlet of Jamaica Bay extending
several miles into the low-slung landscape of southern
Brooklyn, was inhabited by the Leni Lenape for untold
centuries and the earliest site of European settlement
on Long Island. It was here, amidst the marsh grass and
mudflats, that one of the largest and most ambitious urban parks in the world was to be created—a coastal counterpart to Prospect Park. Sprawling across 1,840 acres,
Marine Park would be larger than Central and Prospect
parks combined. Announcing plans for the vast project
in January 1928, Brooklyn park commissioner James J.

Browne—a Tammany hack later charged with embezzle-ment—promised to replace the "straggling, irregular wa-terways and swamps abounding in the area" with no less than "the finest park and playground in the Nation." An initial scheme for Marine Park—little more than a golf course and tidal lagoons laced with paths and roads—was prepared "under stress and hurry" by Julius V. Burgevin, a city landscape architect and former florist from Kings-ton, New York.[22] Disappointed, Browne turned to Lay, his Brooklyn Heights neighbor who knew Gerritsen Creek well and had professed a keen appreciation for the estua-rine landscape. "Of the beauty of tidal marshes," he wrote in a 1912 piece for *Landscape Architecture*, "no one who has lived near them and watched their changing color with the advance of the seasons can speak too enthusiastically. They come to have a place in the heart which mountain scenery, with all its grandeur and fearfulness, cannot equal. Nowhere except at sea does the sky become so much a part of one's life, and nowhere is there greater beauty of line than in their curving creeks and irregular pools."

Unlike most of his contemporaries, Lay also understood the ecological complexity of wetlands. "The tidal marsh," he wrote, "is a delicately balanced organism. It has a flora and fauna of its own, and it depends for its life upon the recurring tides, which bring soil and fertility and moisture for the plants at home there."[23]

None of this, however, eclipsed neither Lay's Calvin-ist sense of utility nor his professional ambitions. When Browne offered him the job of transforming the Gerrit-sen littoral into a modern urban playground, he jumped at the chance. "I believe in the greatness of New York," he professed, "in its people and in its future, and it is my ambition to design a park worthy of New York." Lay's plan for Marine Park, rendered in oil on a nine-by-five-foot canvas, was as titanic in spirit as the city itself. Stretching from Fillmore Avenue south to what is now Plum Beach Park on the Belt Parkway, Lay described his park as "a mammoth sports center, patterned after Jones Beach, in part, but destined to eclipse that resort in magnitude and recreational facilities." It would feature bowling greens, picnic groves, lacrosse and croquet fields, 200 tennis courts, 80 baseball diamonds, swimming and wading pools, a skating rink, zoo, golf course, 30 restaurants and cafeterias, a 1,000-seat casino with formal gardens, an open-air theater, and a music grove. The *pièce de résistance* was a football stadium— the largest in America, with seating for 125,000 spectators, or twice the capacity of Yankee Stadium at the time. "Not only will the principal football games of the country be held there," promised Commissioner Browne, "but it will provide a fitting place for the Olympic Games."[24] All this was organized around a great water armature—Gerritsen Creek, bulkheaded now into a channel two miles long and shaped like a giant banjo. On the waters of the Long Canal and Big Pool would be a recreational flotilla of model yachts, racing shells, and sailing canoes. Here, too, Olympic rowing trials could be held. A new Outboard Harbor at Plumb Beach included slips and moorings for hundreds of yachts, while at the park's southernmost edge was the sea itself, with two miles of new beach on Rockaway Inlet anchored by cavernous bathing pavilions—each large enough to handle 12,000 bathers. The great playground would be New York's first park fully illuminated by electric

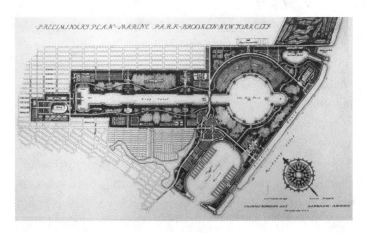

Charles D. Lay, Preliminary Plan for Marine Park, 1931. (Carl A. Kroch Library, Cornell University)

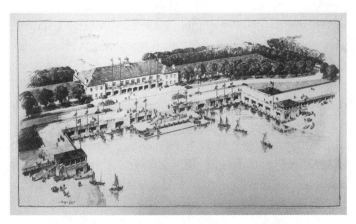

Schell Lewis, perspective view of canoe harbor, Marine Park, 1931. (Carl A. Kroch Library, Cornell University)

lights, enabling it to remain open well into summer nights. Marine Park would thus provide nocturnal diversions of a more wholesome sort than nearby Coney Island, that center of presumed moral mayhem and carnality that kept paternalistic social reformers up at night.

Indeed, Lay's Marine Park plan was a *tour de force* example of the urban park as engine of uplift and reform. This was no place for the *vita contemplativa*, but a mighty exercise yard for the masses—a place of athleticism, gamesmanship, and competitive sport. It was the grand culmination of the playground movement, one that began in Germany in the 1880s and debuted in New York with the formation of the Playground Association of America in 1906. Searching for new ways to fortify immigrant youth against everything from radical politics to exaggerated sexuality, progressive reformers came to see "scientific play" as the solution to a gamut of urban ills. As Dominick Cavallo has written, they considered such recreation "a vital medium for shaping the moral and cognitive development of young people." They believed that structured play would both strengthen bodies and inculcate civic responsibility by exposing youth to "ideals of cooperation, group loyalty, and the subordination of self."[25] Lay had explored solutions to the paucity of wholesome recreation in the city before. In 1927, he and architect Bertram Goodhue collaborated on a center-city architectural precursor to Marine Park—what he called the Indoor-Outdoor Playground. A ziggurat of play, the block-long, six-level structure included pools, playing fields, basketball and handball courts, a dance hall, auditorium, and sun-splashed terraces "easily accessible to mothers with perambulators or with infants in arms." Lay envisioned an Indoor-Outdoor Playground every ten blocks throughout the city's most congested sections and drafted a business plan "to steer a happy middle course between commercialized entertainment . . . and paternalistic benevolence." It would be run by a non-profit corporation—the Indoor-Outdoor Playground Association—that could lease event spaces and ground-level shops to generate revenue. Lay assembled a star-studded board of directors that included Pulitzer Prize-winning playwright Hatcher Hughes, Commissioner of Immigration Henry H. Curran, and city school superintendent William J. O'Shea, and was chaired by George McAneny—a former Manhattan Borough President who would play a major role organizing the 1939 World's Fair.[26]

The playground movement yielded a whole new form of American space—what Galen Cranz has called the Reform Park. It was a radical departure from the ideals that gave us Central and Prospect parks, with their emphasis on leisurely recreation amidst nature as an elixir for urban ills. An ersatz rural landscape in the midst of the city, the old *rus-en-urbe* model might have fortified Victorians against the moral hazards of the city, but it would never do in a metropolis threatened by "the evils which have arisen from congestion of population," as Charles W. Eliot put it. Thus was Lay's Marine Park plan as spatially disciplined as the Anglo-Romantic park was languid and informal. The spatial slights-of-hand that Olmsted and Vaux used to create an illusion of rustic removal from the city gave way now to an aesthetic of probity and pragmatism; sensuous curves yielded to a neoclassical aesthetic of rigid architectonics and axial symmetry. The "discipline of the plan," explained Lay, would bring about an answering discipline in the people, inducing "a sense of responsibility . . . a respect for order and decency that is conspicuously absent in the *habitués* of public amusement parks and beaches." This was a spatial engine to mold the roughest immigrant stock into virtuous American citizenry.[27] It also drew from German precedent, hardly surprising given the teutonic roots of the playground movement. In the summer of 1932 Lay traveled to Germany on a fellowship from the Oberlander Trust of the Carl Schurz Foundation. It was only in Germany—Hermann von Keyserling's tragic laboratory of Europe—that Lay would find "anything approaching play on a large enough scale for profitable study."[28]

Dredging to fill the Gerritsen marshes began in 1931, followed by a formal groundbreaking two years later; the first of 1,200 bulkhead piles for Lay's canoe harbor were driven by Commissioner Browne himself. But then came trouble—and Robert Moses. Construction on the project was being funded through the Civil Works Administration (CWA), an early New Deal initiative plagued by mismanagement and poor planning in New York. By year's end, a lack of building material and machinery idled the 2,000 CWA laborers assigned to Marine Park. Then, in January 1934, Fiorello LaGuardia's fusion administration took the city's helm. In one of his first official acts, LaGuardia appointed Robert Moses commissioner of the new citywide Parks Department. Moses got to work fast, zeroing in on Marine Park—the city's largest park project at the time. His staff found workers there milling about fires, playing dice, and passing around bottles of wine; it was a scene, writes Robert Caro, "more reminiscent of a French bivouac during the Retreat from Moscow than a park reclamation project." Moses fired scores of laborers, then turned to the man whose plans they had been hired to build. It was bad luck indeed that Lay's old nemesis was now in a position of absolute authority over Marine Park. Moses ridiculed "Landscaper Lay" and his lavish park, boasting that "one of the first things I did was toss this ridiculous plan into the wastebasket and get rid of whatever associations there were with the landscape architect in question."[29]

Over the next few years, with Moses heading up the busiest park-building effort in city history, Lay was effectively sidelined as younger, less-experienced colleagues—including former employees—were given plum commissions and influential positions in the Parks Department. But, Lay would have his revenge. In 1939, he led a successful effort by the New York Chapter of the American Society of Landscape Architects to challenge Parks Department plans to run traffic through Washington Square Park, and later helped organize opposition to the Moses dream-scheme of a suspension bridge across the Battery. It was one of the few defeats of Moses's long career. (He crossed the harbor all the same, but underwater with the Brooklyn-Battery Tunnel.) Despite his reserved demeanor, Lay could pull strings when necessary. First Lady Eleanor Roosevelt twice denounced the Moses span— an "eyesore perpetrated in the name of progress"— in her *New York World- Telegram* "My Day" column in 1939, evidently at the behest of "friends on the Heights." On July 11, Lay wrote to President Franklin D. Roosevelt imploring him to stop

the bridge—a "darkening structure" whose "enormous an-
chorage in Battery Park and the placing of the bridge itself
would . . . disfigure our beautiful city." Not a week later,
the War Department canceled the Moses project, despite
previous approval by the New York Army Corps of Engineers—in large part because the new bridge might impede
warship access to the Brooklyn Navy Yard. That it was
a specious argument—there were two older, lower spans
between the Battery and navy yard—itself hints that the
lobbying campaign Lay help lead had struck its mark.[30]

Even without the patronage of Robert Moses, Lay
maintained a busy practice all through the Great Depression and World War II. He still had friends in high
places, if not at the Parks Department itself. Lay's close
friendship with George McAneney, for example, almost
certainly led to his appointment as consulting landscape
architect to the Board of Design of the New York World's
Fair. He was also the landscape architect selected to lead
a large team of designers, plantsmen, and horticulturalists
that created the Gardens on Parade exhibit at the Fair.
He designed the Sutton Square Gardens atop a deck over
the East River at FDR Drive and East 57th Street, and
laid out a factory complex—recently demolished—for the
Scintilla Division of Bendix Aviation Corporation in Sid-
ney, New York, a plant that manufactured engine magne-
tos for sixty percent of American fighter aircraft in World
War II. During the war, Lay drafted plans for Fort Jay on
Governors Island, the Naval Air Station at Floyd Bennett
Field—the city's failed first municipal airport—a Naval
Service Station in Memphis, Tennessee, and a Naval avi-
ation training field in Wilmington, North Carolina. After

Theodore Kautzky, aerial perspective rendering of Brooklyn Battery Bridge ramp through Battery Park, 1939. (From Triborough Bridge Authority, Brooklyn Battery Bridge. Carl A. Kroch Library, Cornell University)

the war, he prepared site and planting plans for several New York City Housing Authority projects, including the Jacob Riis, Sheepshead Bay, and St. Nicholas houses.

For all his skills as a city planner and landscape architect, Lay was also a versatile man of letters. Like the elder Olmsted, he could easily have forged a successful career as an author and essayist. He was prolific and had impressive range, tackling topics as diverse as swimming pools and railroad taxes, woodsheds and art museums, wartime housing, prohibition, and the saloon as "the last great stand of the man's world." His writing is often peppery and contrarian, bucking convention and the status quo.

Charles D. Lay and James A. MacKenzie, perspective view of
Sheepshead Bay Houses, Brooklyn, 1947. (Carl A. Kroch Library,
Cornell University.)

At a time when the patrician American elm dominated
the streets and squares of New England, for example, Lay
championed instead a scorned immigrant—*Ailanthus al-*
tissima or Tree of Heaven. The fast-growing Asian species,
hero of Betty Smith's 1943 novel *A Tree Grows in Brook-*
lyn, was once a popular urban ornamental in cities. But
as American nationalism surged in the mid-nineteenth
century, tolerance for foreign species began to erode. Lay's
own ancestor, A. J. Downing, was shamelessly racist in
denouncing the Tree of Heaven, calling it a "petted Chi-
naman," a "usurper . . . which has come over to this land
of liberty [and] drawn away our attention from our own
more noble native American trees." Lay's position could
not have been more different. "It seems to have a Chinese
quality in its hardiness, its comfortable endurance of trying situations." Its rapid growth and tolerance of brutal
growing conditions—the very characteristics of an ideal

urban tree—instead had stigmatized this eager immigrant. "What can be required of a city tree," Lay asked, "that the ailanthus does not give?" Indeed, it "endures the hardest conditions of soil, drought, drying winds or heat . . . and it is still luxuriantly content and carries itself with an air."[31]

Lay's essays and editorials appeared in many of the most influential publications of his day, including the *New York Times, Herald-Tribune, American Mercury, Pencil Points, The North American Review* and *The American City.* His two books—*A Garden Book for Autumn and Winter* (1924) and *The Freedom of the City* (1926)—mirror the symmetry of Lay's twin life passions of *rus* and *urbe.* The former is as much an exegesis on his love of landscape and nature as the latter is a paean to the city. Lay's prose was clipped and concise; and though a subtle observer of both city and nature, he rarely indulged sentimentalism on either subject.[32] A good example is a poignant essay in which he documented the saga of a baby crow that his children raised one summer in Connecticut. Lay was fascinated with the bird's keen intelligence and penchant for mischief. It would roll stones down the roof in the morning to wake the family up, swoop to one's shoulders when called by name—"Lindy," after the aviator—and tuck bits of boiled egg under the shingles to eat at a later time. "Spools, thimbles, rug hooks kept him constantly amused, and labels stuck in the ground to mark rows of seeds were irresistible." Lay marveled at how the bird would peck at his bare arm—perhaps "unripe carrion to him"—before pondering a reciprocal feast: "I was not . . . without carnivorous thoughts myself and wondered as I felt his plump breast why eating crow is so unpleasant." So domesticated was the creature that it ignored the cawing of wild crows flying overhead. And then one day, Lindy was seen in the apple tree in the company of a fellow bird. He swooped back to share a last meal with his human family before flying off with his new friend, never to be seen again. Lay resisted mawkishly concluding that Lindy had found love among his own. "It is fair to suppose," he wrote instead, "that he was destroyed by the flock he joined, as we ourselves would destroy a traitor or one who became too familiar with devils."[33]

Lay spent his last days at the old family homestead on Chapel Street in the Putney section of Stratford.[34] A stone's throw from Long Island Sound at the mouth of the Housatonic River, he and wife Laura had moved there more-or-less permanently by 1940. It was a homecoming of sorts; if Lay was a New Yorker by choice, he was a Connecticut Yankee by long and deep birthright. The family patriarch, John Laye, had emigrated from London to the Massachusetts Bay Colony around 1648, residing briefly in Cambridge before moving on to the Saybrook Colony in the lower Connecticut River valley. In 1665, he and five other men initiated a "loving parting" from Saybrook to form a new town called Lyme (now called Old Lyme). By the time Charles was born, the Lays had been residing in the town for some two hundred years. Today's Laysville, one of Old Lyme's six constituent villages, is testament to this long tenure, as are the dozens of Lays, Waits, and Ingrahams inscribed on the weathered headstones in nearby Meeting House Hill cemetery. The Putney homestead—"a cheap and mean one in the beginning"—was erected in 1763, built of "hewn oak, mortised and tenoned" and purchased by Lay's father in 1885 as a studio and

Charles D. Lay, watercolor painting of pet crow on a planter, nd.
(New-York Historical Society)

Charles D. Lay (center-left, in white shirt) and family at Wellesmere, summer 1935. Laura Gill Lay is seated at right. Courtesy John Lane (the toddler to left of Charles).

rural retreat. Lay conjectured that it had been built as a boarding house for hired men working the Welles farm.[35] Little distinguished architecturally, save a fine corner cupboard, several fireplaces, and an immense central chimney. Its original clapboarding was nailed directly to the studs "so that the wind blew through quite freely." The furniture inside ranged from colonial heirlooms to yard-sale finds. Outside were ancient rose bushes, trumpet vines, and orchard trees that bore a bounty of Bartlett pears and Baldwin and Russett apples. To the north were views of the Housatonic and distant hills; to the south, the river and Long Island Sound. A discarded privy, salvaged by Lay's father from the local school district and "richly ornamented with erotic school boy carvings," stood in a corner of the garden. Lay inherited the property in 1904, shortly after his mother's passing. Over the next half-century, he added to, deleted, and otherwise altered the house and its grounds and gardens until it was an embodiment of sorts of the man himself—and, all things considered, a fine and tranquil place from which to part this world.

The Freedom of the City

By Charles Downing Lay

I

*I*T IS AS EASY TO SPECULATE about the life of primitive man as it is to imagine what we should do if wrecked on a desert island, and as futile, for we can know nothing of our ancestors who lived and died leaving no records. Where records have been found they show that people even in the earliest times lived largely in cities.

The pyramids required an enormous amount of human labor and they could not have been built without a considerable city near at hand. Men have never wished to live far from their work, nor was it possible in those days to do so. It was then as it is now: four miles an hour is fast walking, and with a twelve hour day, half an hour each way is as far away as any worker would willingly go for his night's rest. No matter how long it took to build the pyramids, the population at any time must have been large, for such work goes on better with a large gang and indeed is impossible, with primitive tools and machinery, for a small one. The monuments of Yucatan, of Peru, of Easter Island, indicate with certainty the presence of an urban population in proportion to the size of the work. Though our knowledge of the times is slight, we can estimate roughly the population required for any great monument. So many people, so many hours work, so many years, were needed, we may say, and these workers composed the city, which was a necessary consequence of building the monument.

Whether the cities which are to be deduced from the monuments and ruins were complete social units or slave barracks similar to our construction camps makes some difference, but even slaves need food, tools and supplies and require a considerable organization in the nature of a city or a military camp. These construction camp cities have disappeared, leaving few traces, but other cities remain in ruins or after thousands of years are still in existence, as those of Mesopotamia which are gone, or those of Greece which in part remain. From these cities of the past has come all our art, literature, our entire civilization. The Old Testament is pastoral in its interests yet it is reasonable to assume that it was written by people of the town who had an audience.

Whether it be that a degree of civilization beyond the barbaric produces a desire for the permanency and safety to be found in villages, or whether the possibility of remaining in one spot undisturbed gives the opportunity for an advance in civilization cannot perhaps be determined, but it is certain that gregariousness and spiritual advancement go together.

Among our aborigines, the higher culture seems to have been reached by those who found a safe retreat in the mesas of the west, but even our eastern Indians tilled the ground, lived in villages, and had a political organization that was well developed. Such an organization could be conceived only in communities of considerable size.

In Greece, and perhaps before, the city was the state, and we owe to the cities of the past much of the political machinery of today. Our own Republic was patterned roughly after Athens, a city state, and after Rome, which later became an empire ruled by the city.

The city of the past was the centre of the social and spiritual life of the time, but depended for its life on trade as cities do today and as trade has declined or changes so have the cities faded or increased.

Few of the big Western cities were in existence at the time of Christ. Yet several of our cities trace their beginning to the first years of our era. They were, like the older cities, located because of some natural advantage, as at a ford (Paris, London) on a trade route, and grew until they became important communities and were made the see of a bishop, or were strongly fortified. When the fortified town grew people were forced to live outside the walls, trusting for protection to the garrison of the citadel. In time the numbers outside might become so considerable that new walls had to be built to enclose them. This might happen several times but each new ring of fortifications being so much longer than the last it may be supposed that the authorities and leading citizens lamented the growth of the city which made new fortifications and hence probably more taxes necessary. They forgot, as we do today, that with each increase in population, the earning power and the ability to pay taxes of each individual in the city became greater. Every person added to the city adds to the opportunities for profitable business and thus to the value of real estate.

Although cities of some kind have always existed, the great city as we know it today is new. Its ever increasing size has worried many people, so that it has become the fashion to look askance at the city and to regard it as an unfortunate accident of modern life which could be so happily enjoyed in pleasanter surroundings. We cherish the luxuries of the city. We like the ease and we like much of the excitement but we are bothered to have so many people about. With all its delights, the city is full of shocks for the person of refinement, sights that sicken, and contacts with fellow men that make one cringe. It is a constant repetition of annoyances for the sensitive; the clamor of the streets, the interruptions of many people demanding a hearing, the discords in time and place keep his nerves ever on edge. The city lacks, too, much of the sensuous appeal of the country. Its hard pavements do not lead one's feet to stray as do the green pastures of the farm, nor is the muddy gutter of the city as pleasing as the brook slipping over crystal pebbles.

We feel in the city restricted and confined and miss the freedom to roam, to idle, to follow our own way in our own time, for which the country gives us so many opportunities. Appealing as they are, these reasons for a preference for the country are sensuous, or sentimental, or querulous and do little credit to the persons who use them as arguments for choosing life in the country—for someone else!

At bottom the case of city versus country is simple. The choice is constantly made by thousands of people every day. To say that those who choose the city would be better off if they chose the country is futile, and not borne out by any of the facts.

It has never been shown by convincing argument that the great city is not the best place to live. It may seem wrong that people in the city (especially you and I) should be deprived of that which is so plentiful in the country, namely space. If space is more pleasing than companionship to some people, it is also more easy for them to secure. But not in the city, for the great merit of the city is in the immense congregation of people in one small spot.

Statistics and experience prove that city people are better off than those who live in the country, in health, in opportunity to make a living, in education and in the possibility of a spiritual awakening. The value of the city cannot be measured in terms of material things only for we must believe that it is only progress toward a higher spiritual life that counts. Our advance in material welfare is nothing so long as we produce no intellects superior to those of Greece. Failing in that we must conclude that there has been no progress in the spirit of man for two thousand years. All else is of little value. The city, however, should be credited with a great influence in raising the average of education and perhaps of intelligence and with a general quickening of mentality, which may in time produce great intellects.

It is evident that our advance in science, in invention, in trade, which makes life today so easy and so pleasant, has made the city possible, as the city in turn has furnished the rich soil and the perfect climate to stimulate the growth of science and invention. The activity of mind which makes the city possible is itself fostered by the city. There is an interdependence so complete between the modern city and scientific progress that they cannot be separated. We might almost say that they are identical and that the city is only scientific and inventive mental activity.

I believe, too, that the city has the same identity with

artistic effort of every kind and that the Muses today dwell on one of our steel framed peaks in the city. It is obvious that many intellectual and artistic activities can only be undertaken in a large city and that the opportunities for the enjoyment of all the things of the city, that is undertakings which require associates or the atmosphere of companionship, increase directly as the size of the city. No argument is possible here. If we care for churches, music, art, literature and the drama, we can have them nowhere so easily and of such high quality as in the city.

There are within a thousand feet of 42nd Street and Broadway, New York, 56,000 seats in theatres and in the whole city 96,000 seats.[1] I can occupy one of these seats any night I please, and if I withdraw my support for years, I can after that time begin again and probably have a wider choice. In a small town if one wants good things one must support them; here they continue without my support.

The city of the present, though its people reach a higher average of education than we have known before, is no less dependent on advantages of site than formerly, but it is on rather a different basis. The cities of the Mediterranean basin were on harbors, or, if inland, on passes through the mountains, or on rivers, but always on trade routes where valuable supplies or manufactures were transported overland. The modern city has no such necessity to be on inland trade routes, which cover the earth like a net and can be rearranged at will. It must have a harbor, if it is on a seaboard, but its prime requisite is fuel or power and raw materials of various kinds.

There are cities which have grown up around a water power and continue to grow because of the inertia natural to cities, even though the water power is today such a small part of their power needs as to be unimportant to them. Such is the case in the Naugatuck Valley and other places in New England which may some day be supplanted in their own specialties by towns more favorably situated in relation to power and supplies. Pittsburgh is a striking instance of a city located on a trade route. It is at the head of navigation on the Ohio River and was a considerable town before coal was discovered under it. It is Pittsburgh's coal and its nearness to good iron ore which made it for a time the chief iron and steel producing city. Its supremacy has been challenged by other towns and Pittsburgh may some day be gone. It would puzzle one to find a site more unsuitable for a great city than that of Pittsburgh. It is at the junction of two swift rivers subject to floods, on a tongue of land with steep hills rising all around. There is no chance for growth past the rivers and the terrain throughout is difficult and discouraging to the city builder.

Boston owes its growth to its harbor. Hartford and Albany were on trade routes. Buffalo was made by lake navigation and the Erie Canal. Many Western cities were trading posts, places easy to defend from attack, or they were on overland prairie schooner routes. The conditions which determined their location have ceased to be of any importance, yet the cities remain as do Paris and London because of an inherent suitability in the site independent of the causes which determined their original location.

Gary, Illinois is one of the few sites deliberately chosen for a city though there are many in Canada along the lines of the Transcontinental Railroads. The influences determining the location of a new city have not been the same since our industrialization. Labor is sought more than power, but since labor too is to be found on routes of commerce, the city is likely to be there.

The moderns city is the direct result of the invention of the steam engine and its use for transportation. It is about a hundred years since the first railroad trains were run and during that time the city has grown steadily while the population devoted to farming has declined.

Steam transportation has made it possible for cities to grow with amazing rapidity. The limitations of time and distance which tended to keep inland cities within certain bounds were suddenly obliterated. Instead of the lines of horses and oxen laboriously drawing food and goods to the city over crowded roads, they were moved swiftly and easily by steam power over rails. With the changed limits of time and distance there came new opportunities for labor due to the application of steam to other work.

The cost of hauling supplies to the city which was high with horse drawn vehicles was suddenly reduced. The uncertainty of water transportation was at the same time eliminated by steam boats. The simultaneous beginning of manufacturing (or industrialization) with its new demand for labor and the development of steam transportation which left idle many teamsters and sailors, as well as the workers who depended on their activities, involved a considerable shifting of population from old country jobs to new occupations in the city. This tremendous change opened a new era, as important in the history of civilization as the discovery of America. It is not alone the ease of communication brought about by steamboat and railroad transportation which has made the big city possible.

Railroads were responsible also for opening our fertile prairies and placing at the doors of the cities throughout the world the cheap and abundant food which was raised there. Every improvement in the method of carrying people, as we might say, in bulk has made another extension of the city possible. Vertical transportation in elevators was a great spur to the growth of New York. The horse car, cable railroad, and elevated railroad increased the effective radius of travel, which was again increased when these lines were electrified. Electricity obviously is not power but only a means of transporting power to small power units, moving or still. Electrification of railways made rapid transportation in subways possible and the limits of numbers of passengers and rapidity have not been reached.

The combination of all the circumstances due to the invention of steam power, electricity and other mechanical improvements and every detail of these inventions such as steel framed buildings, are factors contributing to the rapid growth of the big city, and for our being embarked on an enterprise the end of which cannot be foreseen.

An effective limitation of city growth can only be brought about by the prohibition of steam and electricity. Preposterous as this seems it is quite within the range of fanaticism, and within the range too of the thought of the fundamentalists, who may at any time make a religious issue of the city and decide that since people like the city and are happy there, it must be bad for them. Every one then will have to go back to the simple life of the Old Testament and all modern inventions will be destroyed. We cannot keep part and destroy others. All must be kept or all be destroyed.

In spite of the glory of the cities through the ages and of the praise of its lovers, it needs defenders, needs propagandists and needs devoted thought to make it in the next few hundred years reach our high ideals. The big city as we see it today is a child of the last hundred years; an infant as it were, and to say that it cannot attain maturity is to refuse the hope of the next four or five centuries.

If it cannot, as a political, industrial, and social organization, reach a fertile maturity, and provide the best environment for spiritual and intellectual pursuits, we should end it, but I think the history of past ages shows clearly that the city has been the defender of the spirit.

The rapidity of the city's growth since the invention of steam, and the fact that it is the child of transportation should not be allowed to obscure its existence through all the years as a social institution. Cities are still as they always have been the leaders of thought and of fashion. The intellectual activities and the opinions of Paris, London and New York are matters of great concern to the furthest reaches of civilization. The people of Alaska, of Tasmania, of the Cape of Good Hope, read our books and newspapers and try to keep up with our fashions.

The city is the center for all uplift. The reform of trade, of customs, of manners; the physical welfare of people and the improvement of living conditions all originate in the crowded centers of population, where minds receive a new stimulation from contact with others. Modem civilization as expressed in city life has been accused of shaping every personality in the same mold. Because people live alike and dress alike they are supposed to think alike, so prone are some to take the outward gloss for the inner light. The fact is that city people find great spiritual freedom in an easy compliance with outward forms and fashions. We never know what fiery rebel, what flaming spirit of artist or liberator may be hidden under the correct business suit of the city man.

Picturesqueness in dress is no longer required of the genius nor does it help him in separating himself from his fellows. He finds the isolation and freedom which he needs in following the habits and assuming the costume of the flock. It is a different but more perfect kind of protective coloration.

If the city as a social institution has not the dignity or the stability of the church it has perhaps an equal power for good. Without creed, without legal recognition of its moral supremacy, its efforts for leadership, for spiritual health, for physical well being, are unceasing and its ideal is always the highest of the age. It is kindly and humanitarian in all its effort.

In the city we combine our forces to gain at slight expense many advantages. Think, for instance, what a yell from a city window will bring. First a policeman, then firemen, and an ambulance with its doctor and nurse. What use is it to yell in the country?

For nothing except the rent we pay we can enjoy all the advantages of well-paved streets, which allow us to walk in comfort in almost any weather, all the while being entertained by a procession of people variously interesting. Our children go to schools which are palatial in their appointments, and we can ourselves go to museums to see works of art which are known to country people only in photographs. There are few books one wishes to see which cannot be found in our libraries, but best of all we have in the city a likelihood of meeting people who share our likes and dislikes and with whom we are always happy to talk, and these reasons are no less compelling to an ordinary laborer than to an intellectual.

For thousands of years city dwellers have combined in a more or less unorganized communism, and as the cities grow in size the demand for further enterprises undertaken in common increases. In the most primitive town there is considerable advantage in the protection given by one's fellows, in the borrowing of tools and supplies, in the ability to have some service done by another.

We realize sometimes that police, firemen, hospitals and ambulances are enterprises undertaken in common, but we of New York are likely to forget that our water supply, which is probably the purest and most plentiful in the world, is owned by the City and operated without private gain. Sewers, street cleaning, removal of garbage and ashes are great municipal enterprises for the common good. There are other things for which we pay nothing directly or pay a small tax, but many things for which we pay a small charge are no less due to the fact of our living so compactly. The milk and papers, ice, groceries and meat delivered at our door, the electric light or gas or power, the stream of trains, trolley cars, buses and taxicabs, are all eminently convenient but can be enjoyed by the individual only when he is one of a great mass.

It would be endless to go through the list of things we are able to enjoy at will because there are so many of us; things that few could ever afford for themselves alone and in solitude, we can take or leave.

It must never be forgotten that there are 6,000,000 people in New York because all of them wish to be here.[2] None are held in slavery, except to their own desires and none would leave if given the opportunity. They may talk in a maudlin way about the charms of country life, but they are not serious. Our city houses are likened to those of the cliff dwellers, and our streets to canyons but that is only a picturesque way of saying that we admire them. In a tenement house one has many advantages—solitude which can be ended at will, help nearby in case of trouble, and an entire absence of responsibility as regards the outside of the house; often a communal heating plant and free and plentiful hot water. Few farm houses are so comfortable or so well heated and ventilated. Old tenements, with their many bad features, were shocking but they are fast disappearing. It is objected that city life is a dull grind, especially to the worker, but it often seems doubtful if factory work is as objectionable to the workers as it appears to the sympathetic observer. If one must work, the factory seems better than digging ditches, better perhaps than scrubbing floors, or doing the family wash, for in the factory one is kept warm, one has companions and a definite function in a world which outside the factory seems disordered. There are towns in New England where several generations have worked in the same factory with no apparent unhappiness.

I have already spoken of some of the free things we find in the city as a result of our living together, and we know that these are constantly being increased and the standards raised in old ones. Street cleaning never satisfies us, yet never has the snow been so quickly and efficiently removed as in recent years. We are, too, demanding stricter enforcement of local ordinances which tend to prevent things objectionable to the sense of smell, sight and hearing. Hospitals and schools are all the time improving, as does also the quality and quantity of water, the paving of streets, the decoration of public structures, squares and even subway stations. We are quite properly demanding more and better parks and playgrounds, streets, trees, public baths, beaches, swimming pools and golf courses. Our music and art, if not wholly free, are subsidized to an extent which makes them partly free; but free or not, museums, opera and the theatre can only be had in large cities, and only in cities like New York can one find the variety in cultural interests which we know.

II

*T*HERE IS ALWAYS TALK AND COMPLAINT of New York's congestion. We protest against it, we think we suffer because of it, we say we abhor it, but are we not, when we talk, really boasting of it and unconsciously revelling in it as in some unholy pleasure? But why unholy? Why view with alarm anything so natural, so desirable. The debt limit is reached and we can borrow no more for subways! Well, what of that, if true? We can raise the debt limit or assess the costs on the property benefited if we want to. I, for one, find it every year more worth while living here and I can endure paying for it. This is the crux; how much congestion are we willing to pay for? and in what way must we pay? Congestion, as it is called, is what we came for, what we stay for, what we hunger for. On congestion, if we have power and can move our supplies and manufactures, we depend for our living. Why limit it or ourselves?

At present there is some restraint placed on our congestion. We have limited building to protect one owner from the greed of another and we say "so high you can go with your building, no higher; so much of your lot can be covered, no more," and for a time we restrict the use of buildings to protect the owner of residences of one kind or another. To this limit of congestion we are building. It is a calculable amount. We can say with little error that in any block the day time population will be so many people who must be transported within thirty or forty minutes from this block to their homes between the hours of five and six at night and returned to work between eight and nine the next morning. The maximum population of a residential block can be calculated with the same accuracy.

We are, too, likely to put other limits on congestion by fixing the city plan in advance, determining more closely the proportion to be left in parks, the area necessary for streets, and the population per acre, but I doubt if we will find it advantageous to reduce the limit far below the present condition in Manhattan which is about as follows:

Population 1920	2,284,103
Population per acre	162
Population per acre of park	1,523
Percentage of total area in parks	10.2

Our typical gridiron street plan has as a minimum nearly one-half as much in streets as in the blocks, or one-third of the total area, but the area of streets as built is greater. An open development such as that of much of our outlying districts and suburbs requires from one-quarter to one-fifth of the area or less in streets which as a little consideration will show, means either wasted space in the middle of the block and the same population covering a larger area or a population per block which would be too great for the streets. Our present lot size 16 2/3 feet to 25 feet wide by 100 feet deep has proven economical and convenient. Our block size, too, when it is sometimes varied by additional avenues as on the East side seems about right.

It is customary to make fun of New York's plan, and it has indeed some unfortunate details, but on the whole it fits our needs better than many others. The arguments against it are not conclusive whereas its economy and advantage is great. The excess of east and west streets as compared with north and south may, as the city grows, be found advantageous. The larger blocks and narrower streets of Philadelphia, the wide spaces and enormous blocks of Washington, would not be so good for a city of workers. Nor can Philadelphia, because of its plan ever offer such conveniences as New York. One wonders sometimes if the secret of our great growth is not partly in a plan perfectly adapted to congestion, which produces so much in convenience at a comparatively low cost in money? It is the fact of dividing the costs of streets, with all their service of sewer, water, gas, electricity and unequalled rapid transit among so many people that makes the big city possible.

If we imagine a house 80 feet front, four families to a floor, 10 stories high, we have one family for each 2 front feet, or, if there is a similar building on the other side, one family per running foot of street. Obviously this makes the cost per family low as compared with the suburbs, where each family may have a frontage of 25 feet or more. Some may object that the cost of going up in the air to get room for so many families is greater than a longer street. It may be so, but if we spread out, each person must, because of this spreading, walk further to a rapid transit line, take longer in getting to work or to play, and thus pay in time and inconvenience what he saves in money. The same objection can be urged against a plan for rapid transit lines in a wide parkway. Our many decked streets are great time savers.

There is little doubt that we have carried congestion too far in some directions. The old law tenements were atrocious but it may well be that they were bad not because of the number of people per acre, but because they were bad as buildings. We may conclude that the present law should be revised to limit further the amount of lot area to be covered by buildings, but there is no determinable rule for finding the density which should be prohibited. It is easier to work the other way and find that a diffusion beyond a certain point defeats some of the advantages of the city. A population of 27 families per acre (Sunnyside in Queens) would not permit our subways to make a profit on a five cent fare if the district were large. With this population all conveniences are harder to reach and the cost in time and money is greater. This interesting experiment in housing can last only as long as the restrictions.[3] When these terminate the property may be too valuable, because of its favorable location, to remain so thinly populated. If the restrictions were unlimited in time and the block centers which are now common playgrounds deeded to the city, the houses might remain until the character of the surrounding buildings make them unendurable to live in. In any case it is doubtful if the city would find it profitable to maintain a sparsely settled oasis in the midst of density, or if the district could afford to pay its rightful share of improvement assessments. It may be that a population of that sparseness will find the taxes carried by adjoining property which is unrestricted, too onerous to bear.

The farm laborer or even the farmer himself is not so well housed as the city worker. I have seen many houses in the country worse than the worst in the city, and in general living is not so good. In any comparison between city and country we must compare the worst with the worst—the Negro cabin of the south with the Harlem tenement of New York. I cannot see that the fresh air and hook-worms of the country have any advantage over our Negro district. The Englishmen who come here are shocked by our tenements and wish our working classes could be housed in cottages. Apparently the English notion is that the workers should be like the contented peasantry of old. The idea of Goldsmith, of a "bold peasantry, their country's pride," persists but slightly modified to suit things today.[4] I never believed in the contentment of the English peasants; too many of them left for a better land and ceased to be peasants as soon as they got here.

Congestion in our multiple dwellings is often spoken of as a terrible blot on civilization. But is it? Are not our new tenements warm, light, airy? It is doubtful, I think, if people have ever in the history of Western civilization been so well housed and so free from the accidents and inclemencies of weather or had so little of their time occupied in mere conflict with the elements to keep body and soul together. The congestion of many people living in one room cannot, I suppose, ever be prevented. It is as bad in the country as in the city, and in either case is most likely due to some mental infirmity of the family.

Congestion of homes is a different problem from

congestion of business or theatres. Our theatre congestion is wholly accidental and may soon disappear. The theatre district is the unlovely child of our first subway, opened in 1904 (which was also the beginning of the era of the automobile) and not enlarged until 1918. During that fourteen year period no theatre could exist off the line of the subway, for the subway immediately enlarged the possible patronage of the theatres. The theatres had been on Broadway, almost reaching 42nd Street which became an important station on the subway. They were naturally enough ready to move further up Broadway and they found there a district undeveloped and ripe for improvement.

The path of least resistance was soon crowded but conservatism keeps the theatres there and keeps new theatres from being built in more convenient places. Conditions in the subway, on the sidewalks and in the streets are daily becoming worse so that many people are deterred from going to the theatre because of the delay and discomfort in going or coming whether they go in subway, taxicab or private limousine. Some day the theatre district will of its own volition decentralize or diffuse. The first move perhaps will be the rapid growth of a new district in Brooklyn, Harlem, Queens or the Bronx. The removal of the Metropolitan Opera House to 57th street is a timid choice.[5] Any concentration artificially produced like the theatre district will, when conditions change, automatically diffuse itself.

The convenience of living and working together is as true of theatres as of any other business or profession but theatrical people must forego some of this convenience for the sake of their patrons.

One of our troubles is that the city is growing and we

have not started improvements for the undeveloped territory and some areas built before the passage of the Zoning Laws are built too compactly, but we should not go to the other extreme and think that a city all waste spaces would be good for business.[6] There is a limit to the width of a street as there is to the size of a square or park, and that limit seems to be determined largely by our indolence. We will not cross a street that is too wide, but provided there is a sufficient population back of it, the shops might be duplicated on each side.

None of our idealistic schemes for control of the city are creative. They are restrictive, or ameliorative, but they carry no conviction. We build to the limit of our laws in New York, and deserting the private house we crowd into multiple dwellings and are happy about it.

No one can say what the limit of size of the city may be, for it is a matter of juggling figures, of definition and of boundaries. New York has 5,873,356 in an area of 201,446 acres. London 7,476,168 in an area of 443,449 acres. But why in this computation should New York stop at the Hudson? In the metropolitan area of New York within a radius of 30 miles there are more than 8,000,000. New York, New Jersey and Pennsylvania have 22,261,184, one-fifth of the whole population of the United States.[7]

The city population is more than half of all the people in the whole country, but who can say whether this is too much or too little? It indicates only that we seem to have reached a degree of urbanization. In a day's journey from Boston to Washington; we pass through eight states having a total population of 29,548,239, much of it in the small strip of country along the coast. Yet in three-quarters of an hour by train from any point on this line one is in the wilds and can be almost as free as the Indian of three hundred years ago.

What more could a man with a taste for wild life ask? Nessmuk, the old woodsman, describes a trip through the wilds of Wisconsin, and lived to lament its settlement, but one might with equal sense lament the discovery by Columbus. How far back toward 1620 do we wish to go? The aristocrat will say to stage coach days; the bloodthirsty to the time when bounties were paid for scalps. All have a special hankering for some one picturesque feature of the past; but is there one who would, if he could, turn the hands of time back to pre-automobile days? or go back to 1850 without modern plumbing?

Novelists have often looked ahead and they may in time be thought prophets. I haven't read Bellamy's "Looking backward" since it was published, but I imagine it would seem old stuff. So it is with Wells and perhaps the early parts of "Back to Methuselah."

Statisticians see in the figures of population for cities a rapid accretion, then a slowing of the rate and say "Ah, this can't keep up. The point of saturation is being reached," or borrowing more fantastically from chemical phraseology "congestion reaches the point where the mass must congeal and become stationary." I do not know what this may mean but I think the idea is that a given territory becomes filled up, and after the first great rush, the possibility of finding a place to live is less. It is a condition ultimately unavoidable, never objectionable, and always sought by the business man or the real estate operator. The population of Manhattan Island has decreased 339,074 in the last five year period and probably will decrease further.[8] Manhattan below 135th Street is destined to be the business center of the whole Metropolitan area. The increasing needs of Federal, State and City Governments as well as of great corporations, for office space means a continual replacement of small buildings by large ones and the tearing down of single or multiple dwellings to make room for offices, lofts, apartments, or hotels.

New York will probably always maintain its prestige as the center for fashion, for culture, for art and music. The retail shopping district will grow without ceasing and the manufacturers who supply these retail shops must be near by. Fashionable goods cannot be made by people out of touch with fashion. New York's business is world wide and out of all proportion to the people who live in the district. This must be true of any city and indeed it is one of the compelling reasons for a city, but New York excels all others in America in its attractions for world wide trade. No one who advances beyond the most rudimentary needs can be completely satisfied in the cross roads store. For some things he must go further, to the nearest village, the next city, or the great metropolis. I can see nothing alarming in this tendency. If no one lived on Manhattan Island, but all found a comfortable home somewhere else and went to the little Island only for work or play, it would be quite all right since it is only carrying specialization and efficient organization to a reasonable point for a population of many millions.

Brooklyn and Queens and Richmond [Staten Island] can grow, but only slowly since they have even now reached the capacity of present subways. Opening more subways in their undeveloped territory will bring a tremendous boom in building and an increase in population. Lacking subways enough, the people who would naturally live in New York go to the suburbs, because of more comfortable transportation. But a growth of population in the suburbs should be counted with New York, for the people belong there. Does anyone suppose that Mount Vernon, New Rochelle, Yonkers, Montclair, the Oranges, have grown of their own vitality? They are simply overflow cities of people crowded out of New York.

New York's growth is limited politically by state boundaries but I can see no other limitation except rising costs of fuel, (or power) and handling of freight.

Electrically transported power and a complete reorganization of Port and Terminal facilities are the prime requisites for the growth of New York. If these be looked after there is no limit to our growth, for all else can be paid for on the ground of convenience and comfort. If work is plentiful we can pay anything to live here, but if it fail, New York would disappear like a morning mist.

Some have thought that the city might be limited in its growth by the cost of food, but that seems unlikely for all large cities get their food from the ends of the earth. One can live so far as food is concerned more cheaply in city than in country, in spite of the great conveniences we demand in the handling and delivery of food, which are part of the city cost.

Next to limitation of size or of population per acre as a panacea comes decentralization. Some experts who are astounded by present costs of city operation say that all this ceaseless transportation must be restricted. Probably these same experts would have been astounded by the city budget in 1850. At any rate, they propose to bring about a reduction in traffic by decentralization. In effect they propose a return to the time when everyone lived over his shop and did not clutter the streets by his presence on the way to work. We can imagine the sunny factory surrounded by the homes of contented workers who buy their goods and food at shops near the dressy little civic center, where the school, the church, the town hall and the movie theatre are suitably disposed for convenience. Few of these happy people would ever board a trolley car and much trouble would be avoided.[9]

But will the worker like it? If he changes his job must he move? I fear there is more virtue in the theory than the practise of decentralization. It is a pleasing feature of New York that people can live where they like and are not bound to move with each change in the location of their job.

There is in New York a marked decentralization taking place in certain features and coincidently with the great concentration at its center. Retail trade of the local or daily need variety which is scattered in many districts large and small throughout the city furnishes a good example. Anyone who has seen Broadway or Fulton Street, Brooklyn, or 125th Street or Grand Street, Manhattan, knows that any one does the business of a large city and that each is growing. As these centers which were once separate towns but are now indistinguishable in the mass of the city grow, others spring up and become important, for there is always a necessity to have shops for household needs near the home and these tend to congregate on one street.

Decentralization in wholesale trade or in general business has no merit, for the convenience of being near one's friends and competitors is great and congestion is what we want. The bankers, of course, cannot be far from Wall Street. The metal trades congregate on West Street. Leather is in the Swamp. The jewellers in Maiden Lane. There is concentration even in buildings, as in the Architects' Building, the Doctors' Building, and a man of one profession is uncomfortable and feels out of place in a building full of other trades or professions.[10]

Artists notoriously flock together and create an atmosphere so attractive to the philistine that the artists are finally crowded out to seek new quarters. Artists like congestion in buildings and in districts, and foreigners are slow to diffuse themselves through the city but prefer to go with their own kind.

Parks often do much to separate districts and bring about a partial decentralization, but they must not be placed so as to destroy the great advantage of city life—concentration.

No one has as yet thought much about improvements and changes in the city which might intensify its obvious virtues and at the same time make it better and more pleasing. Town planners who should look ahead and imagine new schemes have devoted all their energies to thinking up plans to mitigate the city; wishing to have their cake and eat it too. They realize that some city is necessary, since we could not all go back to a rural life today.

In England they have invented the garden city, which is an arbitrary limitation of population on a definite area. They propose a city which will be so large and no larger and will always be surrounded by a belt of farms. It is an idealistic scheme so far not greatly productive, and always open to the gravest objections, social and economic.

Garden cities are like our residential districts in suggesting a social order based on land restrictions and a special privilege to live luxuriously in a community so closely controlled that there is no room for the poor, but only for the socially inferior household servant. This may explain why it is so difficult to get servants in the suburbs of our large cities.[11]

The plan may have merit but it limits all advantages to those which are profitable for a small community. It limits the opportunities for employment and for buying as well as for culture and amusement. It is an artificial and deliberate creation of small town ideals for the sake of garden spaces and has, aside from its being a limited stock company, little to recommend it. Is it not a low ideal that grubbing in the garden fits one to exercise the franchise? I have never seen any difference in moral qualities, in the attitude toward home or toward neighbors except in favor of the city.

Nor is there much gain in surrounding a city by an agricultural belt. Though this may save some transportation of food, it cannot save much, for the food of even a small city requires a large farm area. Nearness to market is not a farm advantage as compared to cheapness of production. Most of our food is easy to transport. It is only the perishable things which are best produced nearby, but these when out of season we get from Florida. Actually we increase the cost of all transportation, including that of passengers, by isolating the city since everything must be hauled through the agricultural belt.

Raymond Unwin quotes Lord Bryce as saying "that he knew of no advantage offered by the very large town which could not equally be enjoyed by a town of 100,000 inhabitants" and "later in life he put the most desirable figure even lower, from 50,000—70,000." This is true so far as the simple comforts of life are concerned, gas, electricity, telephones, good pavements, sufficient shops, can all be had in a city of 100,000 people though the cost of these facilities is likely to be higher, but the spiritual and intellectual advantages of the big city are lacking. There are many charming towns, having all the delightful aspects of a garden city, which offer little beside these modern conveniences. It is certain that they give comparatively few opportunities for employment, and that advancement in position is slow or unlikely.

There is a common superstition that ownership of land tends to make a conservative citizenry but I think it would be hard to prove. There are probably as many foreclosures of mortgages in the country as there are dispossessions for non-payment of rent in the city. If you pick a thousand people at random in the city and another thousand in the country, I think you will find the same characteristics in the same proportion in each thousand. People taken in the mass do not vary. There will be the same number of shiftless, ne'er do wells, the same number of average people and the same number of careful, conservative, save-for-a-rainy-day kind, except that in general the more intelligent have sought the larger opportunities of the city.

We are not as attached to the soil as the French are supposed to be and we are always ready to pull up stakes and go on to fresh fields. Some people regret this, but others see in it the working of an adventurous spirit always ready to try new things.

We have not lagged behind the rest of the world in devising political machinery and legislation for improving city conditions, but greater advance will be made through inventing new ways of doing old things, than by restrictive legislation. A good example of such legislation is our comparatively new zoning scheme, which in so far as it protects the rights of individual property owners is admirable, but it may prove to be an obstacle to growth and a disappointment to the many small towns which have sought it as a panacea for all their ills. Too close control may be worse than none at all and end that elasticity and mobility of development which is characteristic of our individualistic ways. The fluidity of our life in its relation to its locus startles the European, who is accustomed to having everything set like a stream of lava which has cooled. Our warm mobility, though it entails some waste is more easily turned into new and promising directions.

"Satellite City" is another fancy term to indicate the advantages of decentralization, but like many others it merely names a condition already recognized. It is supposed to be a city sufficient to itself in most things but depending upon the Metropolis for others. The cities of Westchester and New Jersey are satellite cities, but what does it signify? Some day they will be lost in the mass of New York and of little more importance in the whole than Greenwich Village, Yorkville, Harlem, Williamsburgh or Long Island City.

Foreigners are often shocked at the way we tear down to build again and it seems wasteful to them and avoidable.

Perhaps some of it is, but much of it is a consequence of our rapid growth, of our quite recent development of rapid transit, and of its deficiencies. It will be less in future as our transportation becomes more complete, for it is transit that has developed, changed or destroyed whole districts of the City.

In a recent conference report "A Plan for the State of New York—Planning Problems of Town, City or Region," it is stated that "cities, such as New York, have already passed the limits of efficiency." This is only an opinion and it has little basis in fact. For some industries and for a few people it may be true, but increasing population, increasing business, and a considerable building boom indicate clearly that New York still grows and still prospers.[12]

The same paper says further "there are new elements that allow of decentralization; the automobile, giant electric power, the radio," but as I shall explain the automobile and giant power are forces of concentration.

The large city has a tremendous advantage over the small one in its nearly inexhaustible and elastic supply of labor. If you start a new industry in a small town you must scour the countryside for workers, but if you start in a great city an advertisement in the papers is usually enough.

What theorist can plot the curve of a city and say at what point in increasing area and population it reaches maximum efficiency? If a small town is a good thing, does it not get better as it grows? When does it cease to improve? Many people would say that New York long since reached that stage but I always suspect them of wishing the other fellow to get out.

What seems to be the fact is that no matter what the

practical difficulties of operating a large city, we live in it because we like it better as it grows larger and gives us all the time more opportunity for work and for play. No matter how urgent the reasons may be for limiting its size, it will continue to grow so long as people desire to be in it. If we can handle our freight and be provided with cheap fuel (power) we need not worry about the other problems.

If we think of the great city as one organism, the Leviathan, as it were, of communities, we shall have trouble to imagine one of 60 millions, for there are insurmountable difficulties in the enlargement ten times of all our facilities. A Grand Central Terminal ten times as large as the present one would be impracticable. The idea that the size must be greater to accommodate a great crowd is, I think, the danger in the railway engineer's attitude as it is the mistake of many city planners. We have not gone so far in city affairs as the railways have, for we do not enlarge our schools to take more children but build more schools. Police and fire departments are still scattered over the city.

When we consider the city as a community of separate individuals like the polyps of the Coral Islands, much of our difficulty vanishes. If a city of 100,000 or so people, such as Albany, requires a railway station of a certain size, then New York should have for the same railway system 60 stations the size of the one in Albany. This at once increases the convenience and reduces the congestion caused by our gigantic terminals. What the maximum convenient size for a railway station may be I do not know. I feel certain that our New York stations have exceeded that size as some of our office buildings have admittedly exceeded profitable size.

There is in all human affairs a certain scale to be held to. An 8 foot door is high enough for anybody. If more people must use the door, we provide more doors not a larger one. In our growing city we must have innumerable more units, not larger ones.

Viewed as an aggregation of small units, the problem of the city becomes simple, for there is no difficulty in imagining a succession of little cities touching each other from New York to Boston or to Baltimore.[13]

The obsession of bigness as if the city must grow equally in three dimensions because it covers so much ground has vitiated much of our study of the big city, which is almost as simple as the hive. When the hive gets crowded a new colony is sent out to form a new city. But it prospers close against the old—it need not be separated by open fields, for the bee is nearly as mobile as we and seeks his provender as far afield as we do.

There is no danger inherent in density of population, for the number of people living on an acre of ground tells comparatively little of the way they live. It is not how many of us there are per acre but how well we live that determines whether the city be well or ill. If people crowd into too few rooms it matters little whether those rooms be in city or country.

III

OWN PLANNERS TALK MUCH OF AMENITIES, a word that they have adopted for their own. But of what amenities do they speak? The amenities of a great city are not those of a small farm. One must choose between them and be satisfied one way or the other. We cannot in the city have the fragrant air of the hay field, the fern clad dingle with its cooling spring, nor can the farmer have our opportunities, our conveniences, our stimulation to accomplishment or our intellectual pleasure.

Is compromise possible? Perhaps, but where? A hint of country of pleasures may be possible in the city, but they cannot be allowed to interfere with the essential quality of the city which is congestion, the convenience of mass operations and economy. Rus in urbe is a fantastic ideal. For more than a very little country in the city spoils some of the advantage of the city.

For the moment and because of eight years of an obstructionist mayor, New York is behind in its necessary mechanical development. We are eight years behind in subway building, almost as much in carrying out the far sighted plans of the Port Authority for the reorganization of commercial transportation and five or six years behind in building a commuter subway from all the suburbs to all the boroughs. The latter plan will bring about a kind of decentralization since it will make any district equally desirable for any business, for pleasure, or for residence. Decentralization is most effectively brought about by giving the traveler on any transportation line a wide choice of destination. A suburban train making six stops at the beginning of its run and six stops in the city at the end of the run and returning making the same stops gives opportunity for wide distribution. Every one of its six stops in this city is as important, for example, as Grand Central Station, which might have been its former terminal. Decentralization of this variety inevitably adds to the congestion of the whole territory and, as I insist, to its amenities, its convenience, and its economy.

A city subway is like a new machine which a manufacturer may buy. He cannot pay for it at once but he knows that the saving through its operation will enable him to pay for it. We can buy any subway, bridge or tunnel if we feel that people will pay in sufficient numbers for its use.

We never reach the point of having subways enough; as new ones are built they are soon used to capacity without affecting existing lines of the same type. We have the riding habit and if there are more opportunities to ride we ride more.

An increase in subway trips and in length of trip per capita is the best possible proof of the popularity and convenience of city life. I frequently make six trips a day: Four for business, (by preference I take two lines each way) and I like the location of both office and residence; two for pleasure, and it is no hardship to ride in the warm and rapid subway on a winter night. It is convenience not necessity that makes New Yorkers so ready to use the many lines of transportation. People who object to the crowded conditions, do not refuse the conveniences offered but are annoyed by the fact that they are used by so many others.

What, we may well ask, will the end be of this tremendous materialistic development? If great things have come from the city in the past, will not perhaps greater ones come from the greater city of the future?

It is in government and in finance that we are most backward, and I wish that some of our people whose chief interest is supposed to be finance would devote themselves to it even to the neglect of the imaginative field of regional planning.

Enthusiastic town planners, having the fear of the city in their hearts, sometimes dream of a country wide distribution of the population. There is no more amusing parlor game than to sit down before the Geological Survey's topographic maps and plan whole regions or whole states. The maps give to the experienced eye a satisfactory picture of the country. One sees the river valleys, natural lines for railroads and highways, the steep hills on which agriculture would be difficult, and the fertile plains where farming should be easy and profitable. The big centers of population are obvious. One connects them with a blue pencil line following the valleys or sometimes, to save distance, climbing and descending a hill. One might go further, arranging minor centers along the road, crossing out the highways which should be abandoned marking forest areas in green, agricultural areas in yellow and built-up sections in purple. Such dreaming can be carried to any length one wishes. Any theory from complete urbanization to an even distribution of so many people per acre, or so many per square mile, can be carried through to the bitter end—on paper.

Town planners have too often taken the attitude of the doctor who sees only sick people and to whom everyone is ill. This has been forced upon them perhaps by circumstances but it is a position which should be abandoned. The city is a healthy growing organism having certain bad habits it is true, but no weakness and no disease. It is not a cancerous growth to be removed nor has it any weakness except (to carry the metaphor further) high pressure and some of its arteries. The town planner must forget his morbid delight in what he pleases to call the ills of the city and approach his work in a more hopeful mood as if he said "this machine is interesting and full possibilities; what can I do to make it more perfect?" His thought and his efforts then will not be devoted to so much rebuilding as to new inventions—new plans for living.

One man obsessed by the idea that anything is better than the big city has proposed a road town, which is, as I understand it, an endless row of houses on each side of a railroad and highway running through open country. In front of the house a city street; at the back door, farms, pastures, forest.[14]

Another idealist would have the city built on concentric streets thinning in population toward the outer rings, with radial boulevards or streets stretching out through the suburbs to the country like points of a star.

Each dreamer has a different scheme and a reasonable theory to support it. Anyone of them could be worked if it seemed worth while and many strange schemes have been successful in this country until they were interfered with from the outside. The Oneida Community, The Mormons, The Fourier Phalanstery, all went well until accident or public disapproval caused them to be in part abandoned. As we look back, few of them seem important and their success would have changed things so much today, that we must be glad of their failure. They had no thought for the individual and were financially successful at the expense of better things.

We are moving in a definite direction and most of us seem to like it. To attempt to change it, making our object a different one, for some theoretical advantage, seems unwise. There are besides too many factors determining our direction for any one mind to grasp. The effort I think should be to get the most we can out of the life which we have and will have in the future. Turning back the clock will not help. We must go on to the end with mechanical development, with our industrialization and with the standardization which they bring.

I do not believe that the dangers are as great as people think or that the discomforts are so annoying. We have already lost much in the history of our civilization. We have lost the God-King of Egypt, The Prophet-King of the Hebrews, the Absolute Monarch, the Feudal System, the Trade Guild, Serfdom, and Slavery. Each appeals in some mysterious way to our desires for pomp and ceremony, for dependence rather than independence, but above all to the rationalistic desire for a well ordered world instead of for one which has the disorder of movement.

The gain which we count against this loss is overwhelming and few who lament past grandeur would be willing to give up present comforts if the opportunity were offered.

The air is full of hopes of new things which are expected to bring about decentralization and definite halt in the growth of the city. Chief among them is the super-power system which will link up all steam and water power plants in the East and send the power countrywide. In theory each farmer will be able to start in any light industry he pleases. The country districts will be, as regards availability of power, equal to the city, and the country machine shop will moreover be free of some of the heavy expenses of the city such as costly building, high taxes, truckage, and high wages.

It is indeed quite possible for a small industry to move into a village and find there cheap power, cheap rent, a railroad siding and a limited supply of cheap and good labor, but as the industry grows it must attract more labor, thus starting a city, or move to a larger city. Either way it inevitably becomes an urban industry.

For a smaller industry, such as any mechanic or farmer might start, the difficulties seem insurmountable in spite of cheap and abundant power. In the first place there is a capital expenditure for motor and machines and the overhead on these. How can he get the capital? No one will invest in an experiment in industry which depends upon the capacity of one untrained man. What shall he manufacture for a country well supplied with everything, and in what quantity, and how shall he market his goods? Any manufacturer knows that the cost of selling goods comes near to equalling the cost of manufacturing them. How much will the small manufacturer be restricted by lack of full equipment? A machine must run continuously if it is to be made to pay, and many machines which are necessary to produce a cheap and perfect product cannot be so run in a small plant. In some industries the by-product saved often means a considerable addition to profits, but by-products can only be saved in large plants. In a small plant it does not pay to save them. From every point of view the small country industry seems impracticable.

Efficient small scale production will undoubtedly come—is here, but only in articles which must be delivered fresh to the consumer. Such things are newspapers and bread, but to these might be added the things done while you wait, like pressing clothes, repairing shoes, and endless work on automobiles. But the amount of power and of machinery needed for such work is little. Any article which is not too heavy to be shipped cheaply can undoubtedly be made more profitably in a big city and sold for less in the small town than if it were made there.

The textile industry is typically one that can be carried on anywhere and is indeed scattered over the whole country. Theoretically a loom could be set up in a farm house and watched by a housewife, but practically the scheme is impossible, for the product of a high speed loom is so great that the capital involved in raw material would be an obstacle. There is besides the difficult question of style, of pattern, of selling, and the possible loss through fluctuating price which again makes it impossible. These troubles have for many years made the cottage industries difficult to keep going. Mills in the South which were started to take advantage of an unexploited labor supply of low quality find it profitable for a time, but this is temporary and they must soon pay standard wages. The freight rate on their finished product to the ports or the distant centers of population will then be an unfavorable factor in their costs.

Undoubtedly the superpower system will help the farmer somewhat, enabling him to grow more with less labor, thus further reducing the rural population. It will undoubtedly add to the size and prosperity of the small towns as well as the large cities, and it may have some influence in shifting an industry formerly held in one place by cheap power to another place nearer its raw material or its market or where other conditions are better.

Nearness to the source of supply is not often a considerable object, for most raw materials are cheap to handle and ship, whereas the finished product must be expensively packed and shipped at much higher cost. Nearness to the market, which saves these shipping costs, is a much more powerful drag and that is all toward the big city. The Bethlehem Steel Company finds it cheaper to manufacture steel on the coast at Sparrows Point, avoiding the long haul by rail of the finished product to seaboard cities.[15] The canning of fish and vegetables are the only industries in which proximity to source of supply is necessary.

The art of Town Planning, of which we have heard so much and are sure to hear more, is not new in this country. Philadelphia was laid out by Penn in 1682, Washington by L'Enfant before 1800, and New York in 1807. The rebuilding of Paris was not started under Haussmann until 1850. Since our early days we in New York have done creditable work which has produced a city quite different from those of Europe, but no less admirable, for in any consideration of town planning one must take the whole city into account, not compare one feature with another but the whole with the whole. Our formal parks and squares are not so good as those of Paris, but the city as a physical organization of water supply, streets, sewers, transit, housing, is far better, and best of all it is in every detail nothing but New York.

The town planning of recent years has been seriously injured by German influence which tends to a carefully studied and dull romanticism. It is a style of twisty streets, accidental and picturesque placing of buildings, a deliberate seeking of medieval sources in plan and in architecture. It is justified on a curious basis of science and art; curved streets are good because they fit curved hills; because they fit natural conditions they are, therefore, beautiful (is not nature beautiful?). One reasons thus when buying a spring suit. English town planners are tainted with the same culture, but even more stupidly. They say as it were, a row of houses all exactly the same is dull; therefore let us break up the row and have them as different as possible; so we have in typical examples a restless change, like a crowd of people watching a parade, all different and all trying to break out of line. Some day a genius will do a whole district in the American style (the so-called Colonial) with blocks of similar houses having a quiet sky line, trees carefully arranged, the open spaces open, and studied as carefully in their shape and size in relation to buildings as the buildings themselves are studied.

If American town planners can do no better than current English and German work in residential districts they might as well quit. If they cannot plan better boulevards, squares and formal parks than there are in France or Italy they will have another reason for giving up the game. It cannot be done by imitating Europe. The fountain of town planning wisdom is not England or Germany or France. It is just as likely to be here; one cannot tell, for town planning is not to be judged by its theories but by its results in creating a great city. That seems more likely to be done here than anywhere in Europe. In the doing we may rebuild New York two or three times more. It has been done at least once in my memory.

Town planning is a matter for many experts, who must work in the greatest harmony with no superior, no power in control. For if you are planning a city where will you start? With streets, laid out by an engineer? Will they then suit the Rapid Transit Engineer? Or the Architect who is to make parks and squares, or the Railway Engineer who must somehow get his freight yards in the best relation to the railway and the city? What, too, of the sewer engineer, the dock builder and the vehicular traffic engineer?

Indeed the modern city is so much of an engineering problem that one is likely to forget that appearance counts for anything. As Werner Hegeman, of Berlin, said before the war,

"The prevalence of artistic ideas in the city planning of past ages and in the much less successful efforts of the last generation can be explained by the fact that the city planning work was done by either architects or landscape architects, both of whom were mainly trained to see aesthetic values. But during the nineteenth century these artists have often been supplanted by surveyors or civil engineers."[16]

Our problem in planning the city is to get the many

engineers to work in harmony and to have with them as an equal partner in the work of each, an artist, whether he calls himself town planner or landscape architect, so that whatever the undertaking, the opportunity for a result pleasing to the eye and gratifying to the senses, and perhaps to the aesthetic emotions be not missed. For it usually costs no more or only a little more to give our work this added value. We must learn that not only buildings but all works can be designed with regard for appearance and will add to the pleasure of our city life in the degree that they are well designed.

This is not a plea for idle and superfluous decoration, which is more distasteful to the artist than to others, but for the application of trained taste, judgment and artistic skill to ordinary engineering problems. In any work in which the artist is consulted it may be that he will add nothing, take away nothing, but by changing the proportions, the spacing, or the location give the work a new and permanent value. The value of such qualities of design and good taste we are fully aware of and willingly pay for in clothes, in furnishings and in our houses. We know that appreciation of such values has saved our colonial City Hall, has prevented encroachment on Central Park, as it has preserved many natural features. There are in New York many accidental beauties and many thrills caused by the simplest of engineering works, but there is not enough of the sensitively felt and carefully executed work of the artist.

There is not in New York a single formal square on which monumental buildings front, which gives any hint of that sense of space, of just proportion, of agreeable decoration and of care in its details which is so much of the charm of Paris. Yet such a thing is no more difficult for us than for the French, it costs no more to do than many of our stupidities and as everyone should know such work adds in dollars and cents to the value of real estate and to the possibilities of trade, in hotels, theatres and shops. When will we stop trusting the planning of our cities to engineers only and give the artist his equal share in the work?

Town planning is not fundamentally a matter of street layout, population, traffic, and other physical things, but a matter of pleasing people who must live and work and are determined to make that life and that work as fine as possible. Our ideal is not a low one of ease, but is one of ambition in many directions, for ourselves and our children. Town planning must contrive to make the city fit the needs and desires of the people, and it must not attempt to create a city to which the people must fit themselves.

The danger in our present condition is that we may be so annoyed by this or that petty thing in the heart of the city that we forget to do the important thing on the outskirts while there is yet time. For the relief of any city today must be found largely in improvements on the outskirts. It is too late to correct some annoyances so let them be accepted and do other things which are more readily achieved. It is of the greatest importance to build more main highways from the city to the surrounding towns, for we feel the congestion of motors more just outside the city than we do within it. Going through the center we expect delays, but when we reach the borders we should be able to move ahead more comfortably.[17]

The amenities of city life might next engage our attention and we should, I think, replan and rebuild and put in order all our parks. Do some house furnishing as it were, and throw away the tawdry stuff of the General Grant period, and replace it with more modem furnishings better adapted to the increased size of our family and to modern methods of housekeeping.[18]

When the time comes for rebuilding there will be many conflicting views, but whatever is done must be done by the artist, unhampered by the statistician with his survey, his traffic counts and his childish conclusions. Nor should the artist be at the mercy of any engineer who might say, "thus and thus should the work be done because it is the practice to do so under these conditions."

The artist is the innovator, the inventor. He does things in new ways, or in old, as appears best, since his purpose is not to justify a theory or a method but to produce a result. It is the artist who knows and cares for the amenities of city life, and he will be first to grasp the possibilities for joy and beauty in our congestion, in our enormous size, in the infinite variety of our physical environment. He will welcome, too, the limitations of that environment, for to him limitations are a spur to greater inventiveness. If, as I think, the collection of millions of people in one spot is productive of good, why should not the adding of more millions be productive of more good? If our opportunities are so great today will they not be greater tomorrow? I feel so assured of the continued growth of our cities and so happy about it that I wonder at the fear of size which is so general. We who remember the first motor cars know that a Cadillac of today would then have filled us with fear of its size and its power, but the fact is that cars now climb trees less frequently and are more easily controlled and safer.[19]

Politically the great city is becoming more powerful, more independent, and is taking to itself through necessity functions which our forefathers never thought of and which we sometimes view with alarm. Naturally enough our political machinery for managing the big city has lagged behind our development in science and invention, but we are progressing and the next step in advance will be, I think, in city government, which must be improved in organization and in technique. The powers of the city government will no doubt be further extended so that it has still greater control of private property, of public utilities, of education and of recreation of any type. Step by step we are marching toward an autonomy which will put the city in control of the State and toward a power which will limit the individual's chance to injure his neighbor but leave him free to enjoy living in his own way so far as his spiritual life is concerned. The physical freedom of yesterday we have forgotten. Who longs for the freedom to throw garbage in the street, and who except the most avaricious landlord wishes for the freedom to build tenements as he pleases and to maintain them as suits him best?

The desire for concentration is seen everywhere, in rural schools which are being abandoned in favor of a central school with larger opportunities, in the decline of the small general store and the increase of mail order houses, and in every industrial enterprise.

We should get over our fear of the city, cease trying to ameliorate it by giving it weak echoes of the country or by making it innocuous by great dilution, but try rather to make this new machine a good one that will work, instead of saying all the time, it is too big, it will not work!

IV

IF YOU LIVE IN THE COUNTRY and must work for a living, where will you find it? On the next farm? If not there, where? What will you do evenings? Have you ever seen a farmer's family and the hired man go through the daily grind and slink sleepily to bed?

Almost any farm must be self-contained. It must have its own complete equipment of livestock, tools, implements; and the farmer must be willing to tackle any job at a moment's notice. He must sometimes shoe the horses, repair the Ford, mind the baby and drown the kittens, all of which things city dwellers may easily have done for them.

There is no way to subsidize the farmer; his fate must in large part be left to economic justice. If he raises too much it will sell for little. If he cannot make it pay on the present basis he must starve or quit. If enough of them quit, prices will rise and those remaining will do better. He cannot control production to any great extent. His plant cannot be shut down. If it does not produce corn, it is hay or ruin. He is often selling his factory product in competition with the surplus of a manufacturer in another line. Thus the poultryman is always in competition with the wheat farmer who has a few chickens that seem to cost nothing to feed and which he is willing to sell for a little ready cash. It is the same with fruit, with many vegetables, even to a degree with beef. Greater production per acre or per hour of labor employed may help the individual farmer for a season or two, but when all farmers employ the same methods, the price is automatically lowered except as greater demand may tend to hold it stationary. The net result to the farmer of better methods or cheaper production is a freeing of more labor for city employment. Since the basic price of farm products has always been fixed by the cost of producing them, the farmer who is a good manager makes a profit, the poor manager a loss. This must always be the case so long as the farmer is independent. Working for an employer, the difference in pay would not be great between the good and the poor manager. The good one would be always employed, changing positions seldom, while the poor one would be often looking for work.

Farming has changed in the last fifty years in a thousand ways. Machinery, as I have said, is the chief cause in reducing the amount of labor needed and has thus decreased the farm population. The surplus labor on the farm is less, since the casuals, the retainers, and the permanently employed who were in number according to summer needs, and had little to do in winter, must now be fully employed the year round and get the same pay winter and summer. This labor cost as well as the reduced supply and large demand has increased the cost of the farmer's fuel and of all the work of keeping up fences, walls, roads and buildings.

The plentiful labor on the farm in former times was one excuse for making many things which added to the happiness and ease of life. Food, furniture, fish nets, clothes, ox-yokes, horse shoes, baskets and eel pots, all used to be made at home, but making them today at present labor prices cannot be done. It costs too much now to send a man to the mill with grain to be ground. However cheap manufactured things may be, the farmer pays two profits on them when he buys. The department of agriculture has taken a paternalistic interest in the farmer. It has urged for his contentment and for that of his family all the luxuries of the city. He is expected to have telephone, electric light, piano, radio, open plumbing, furnaces and all the machinery to make farming easy and housework light, saddling himself with a heavy capital investment and rapidly increasing charges for depreciation.

Schools, concrete roads, churches and town halls add to his pleasure and sometimes to the value of his land. But so long as he remains a farmer, the value of the land he farms means nothing to him except increased taxes and reduced profits. It is indeed a calamity for him as a farmer to have the land increase in price. There are large districts where this has happened and where in consequence little farming is done. The farmer if he remain on the farm becomes in these communities a real estate speculator, holding on with as little cost as possible for the largest price he can get. Around all our cities this has happened and in many popular summer resort districts the price of land is a gentleman's price too high to permit farming at a profit.

It seems a little mistaken to urge the farmer to indulge in city luxuries, when he must miss the intellectual and spiritual delights of the city which do not come to him well over telephone or radio. Is he not being urged to make too heavy an investment in plant and in fancy contraptions which city people themselves soon learn to go without?

A more promising enterprise, I think, would be to persuade him to abandon his feudal ideals for a more useful communism, which might be done without giving up too much of his poetic independence of spirit.

In many parts of the country the farmer and his hands got much of their living free. Abundant fish, clams, oysters, ducks, quail, woodcock, rail and other game birds, and sometimes deer furnished many delicious meals. Much of our farming heretofore has been a kind of exploitation of natural resources, but this period of abundant game, timber and virgin soil has almost passed, and the farmer must work for all he gets.

It is not a fanciful idea to suggest that farming would be most helped by a plentiful supply of game, which could be bagged only by farmers. A region absolutely protected from entry by any casual motor or any non-resident would restore farming to something nearer its old condition of peace and plenty.

Why should the dude sportsman have any rights to game which is wholly raised on farms? If they must have birds to shoot, let them practise on city pigeons. The man who can afford to buy gas for a Packard can afford to buy sirloin steaks.

To restrict the use of fire arms to land owners within five miles of the land they own, where the population per acre is less than a certain amount, and to close the secondary roads of rural districts to all but residents may be thought un-American, but these are reasonable privileges to give the farmer, if he is to be coddled.

Trapping was another source of income which has disappeared, yet with the restrictions of the game laws the farmer often suffers from the depredations of skunks, weasels, foxes, deer, and other vermin, which he is not permitted to kill except when seen doing damage. Why should these vermin and others such as the beaver, be preserved for vicarious naturalists or the casual sportsman of the city?

It will shock many people if I suggest a kind of country club or hunting preserve for the farmer, yet that might go far toward making him contented. If it is good for the city man why not for the hick?

It may be as wise for us to abandon the New England farmer as it is for him to abandon his farm, since he cannot under present conditions compete with farmers in other parts of the country. He complains that the rate on milk shipments to New York is as great as from Canada where land and labor are cheaper and that the site value of his farm is nothing as regards the New York market.

To keep the farm in anything like its old feudal condition with a complete equipment and many retainers can only be accomplished by political action and by co-operative buying and selling. The dependence of the city on the farmer is great, and whenever the farmer shows a reluctance to supply our needs we shall have to offer suitable inducements. For the good of both, the speculation in food which raises prices to the consumer without as a rule helping the farmer but enriching only the speculator should be stopped. Producer and consumer are both too much at the mercy of carrier and middleman.

There is complaint from country employers of the difficulty of keeping labor on the farm, and reproachful remarks about the foolishness of farmers' wives and farmers' daughters in their longing for town life, as if that were a sign of moral weakness. But it is on their part not wholly selfish. They would have for the farmer less drudgery, more human ease, as they would have for themselves wider opportunities and less dulling monotony.

It may be that the farm of the future will be so large that machines can be used to do all the work and all the farm hands will be mechanics, living in a company village and going to and from their work in company buses or in their own Fords. The women then will have opportunities for social pleasures, for factory work, perhaps for more intellectual affairs. There will be no one left on the farm at night except the night watchman. Farming under these conditions will be capitalistic, and those who maintain that the small farmer owning and working his land is the backbone of the country will not like it.[20]

The alternative method of cityfying the farmer is to give him by means of communistic and co-operative enterprises every possible advantage of city life. For complete fulfilment of this ideal it may be necessary to remove him from his own farm and locate him in small hamlets, with houses quite close together and a considerable equipment of library, community hall, church, school, water, sewer, electric light, concrete sidewalks and other conveniences. A doctor and nurse may have to be employed by the community. Even now small towns in New England have offered to subsidize a doctor for living in the town.

It would be an interesting experiment to start such a colony, providing a comfortable village, good roads, the best farm buildings and every convenience for rapid and efficient work. The difficulty is to keep it from becoming too paternalistic on the one hand and too uniform in its social requirements on the other. The eccentric, the loafer, the person with a special vocation has a value and certain rights which might not be recognized in such a compact society as this must needs be.

I know a woman of education and culture who lives with her family on one of our most frequented state highways. They carry on a large business and many people are coming and going within a stone's throw, yet she longs for her old home, which was on a crossroad where half a dozen houses were clustered. There she could in a few minutes run across the street for a chat with a neighbor and be still within sight of her house and her family. As it is now she must walk a quarter of a mile or take the Ford a longer distance to a considerable town. Few people realize, till they have tried it, the loneliness of life in the country or the comfort which it is to a woman to have the reassuring presence of her kind.

Specialization in farming is as much a fact as in industry. There are communities where sheep raising is the common interest; others where all are dairymen with only one breed of cattle; others as we know devoted to apples or oranges or peaches. The general farm raising everything for its own needs is a thing of the past.

Another consequence of specialization is in the use of land, for all realize that any land is best used for a particular purpose. Thus much of it with the reduction in the number of farmers and of farms is reverting to forest, as it should. However profitable they may have been before the railroads were built, many farms cannot be made to pay, and when farming is given up the land returns to forest and its primeval condition. There are many parts of the country where one can walk through thick woods and find tumble down walls showing that there were once fields or pastures there.

The decrease of rural population, as we have seen, is a direct consequence of the use of labor saving machinery. I wish that I knew the production per man of several crops at ten year periods back to 1870. There is no doubt that it has increased enormously, and will continue to increase as the use of machinery is extended to other crops and other operations. I have seen fields of grass mown by hand, the hay made without machinery, and I have seen rye reaped with a cradle, which I judge is a Yankee improvement on the curved sickle of Europe, but I would be put to it to find such an operation going on today. Grain, too, I have seen threshed by hand. After such labor what chance for thought?

The desire for independence in money affairs, for opportunities to advance oneself in whatever interest one has, for companionship and ease will always tend to make the towns grow at the expense of the country, and I believe the movement is even greater than the statistics show, for in every factory town there are many workers living in the country and travelling back and forth every day. They stay by the farm because it is the old home or because of affection for parents or because they are settled and moving seems too great a risk. But they are to be counted as among town dwellers, they have many of the advantages of town life, and they do not want to be farmers of the kind they have known. What attractions there might be for them on a farm if they could be machine farmers I do not know.

The suggestion has been made, following the Florida

boom, that we make an annual migration from North to South and back in large numbers. Perhaps this would serve to break the social fixity of a communal farm. Connecticut tobacco growers have been somewhat accustomed to this migration. The tobacco season is short, the profits sometimes large and the long winter gives little occupation.

The first serious complaints of the concentration of people in big cities was made about twenty or thirty years ago when the abandoned farms of New England were the subject of a considerable propaganda. Many of them have since been bought as summer places for city people but they are only a degree less abandoned than before. The farms themselves are abandoned though the farm houses are cared for and occupied part of the year.

In time, whole states may be nearly deserted and it is within the range of possibility that some of them may be so oppressed by taxation for schools, for roads, and for policing that they will become nearly bankrupt and wish to surrender their charters as states and to have their territory divided amongst their neighbors.

The solitude which summer people like is a hardship to some towns for many miles of back roads must often be kept passable for the sake of a few places which do not pay taxes enough to maintain the roads to reach them.

The demand for perfect roads for motoring has helped to open up the country; and the motor has made places ten miles or more from a railroad station possible to live in, but at the same time it has brought about a dangerous condition on the farms. The farm papers are full of stories of automobile thieves who come with bags and barrels and steal potatoes and other vegetables from the field and fruit from the trees. They steal poultry, calves, cattle and sheep which are butchered on the roadside. Protests from the farmer may end in a beating by two or three ruffians or by a shooting affair. Hunters tear down fences, cut and burn and do untold damage. When someone appears to protest, they hop in the car and are off, no one knows where. Motor bandits are too common in the city but in general attack only those known to have large sums of money. In the country any one may be attacked, so that for safety one's home must be a fortress. The danger of motor banditry no less than the social and economic forces I have mentioned will be a strong reason for seeking the protection of communal life in villages and compact hamlets.

With the abandonment of farms and the collection of the farm mechanics in small settlements there will be few people left at large. There will be lumber men in lumber camps, trappers wandering in the forest and along streams, collecting furs for city markets, and on the shore, fishermen gathering food from the sea.

V

IT HAS BEEN A SUPERSTITION for a long time that city living is not the best living but in spite of this cities continue to grow and city dwellers pretend to yearn for the country. Meanwhile, the continuous decrease in the proportion of country to city population has worried many good people who fear that such a movement is a danger to the nation. The minds of some are obsessed by the physical benefit of fresh air, strenuous exercise and calm nerves. Others think they see in the farmer such sterling moral qualities that the nation would cease to exist without him as a sort of balance wheel on the racing city. They do not think perhaps of the excess of fresh air, the overexertion dulling nerves and intellect, which is too often the lot of the farmer. Nor do these city dwellers who praise country living seem to value the superior mental activity, the quick reactions and the high sensitivity of the city man.

I can think of no great man in our history who was content to stay on the farm. They all sought the nearest town at the first opportunity. Even Thoreau owed much to the companionship he found in the village of Concord and he was not unknown in Cambridge or unfamiliar with Boston and New York. Perhaps the gist of it is that the farm offers considerable advantages as a nursery, but it would be hard to prove by cases that it is any better nursery for genius than the town. A moron may be a marvel compared to a cow, but a real man is only to be proven great by comparison with his kind.

Figures of population showing the drift to the cities in New York State follow: (urban including villages of 2,500

	1900	1910	1920	percent 1920
Rural	1,970,783	1,928,120	1,795,383	
Urban	5,298,111	7,185,494	8,589,844	82.7

or more)

The same tendency is shown for the country at large, which has 57.4 percent urban population in 1920 and 45.8 in 1910.

Why this should worry anyone or be considered as anything but natural I cannot imagine. Perhaps it is a kind of sentimental self-pity that makes city reformers long for country delights. City people in summer time often look with thrills of admiration at the horny handed farmer trudging behind the cows and think of him as a modern Viking.

A young man cannot marry and start farming without capital. He must furnish the house, buy nearly as many clothes as in the city, besides buying all the horses, cows, poultry and endless machinery. And it is to be remembered that he is investing his capital in a business subject to many chances and he may lose it. Paying installments on the separator or the tractor or the continuous expense of keeping up a young orchard may defer for years the purchase of a fur coat for his wife. In the city a boy with a good job can marry at once; no capital is required.

Life in the country, indeed, has its romantic aspects, and gives apparent freedom from the worries of the town. One dreams of fruit from one's own trees, of potatoes won in devastating battle from the soil, of milk arduously strained from the cow, of the barrel of cider hardening in the cellar. The landlord, if one can buy a place, does not come around. But are not visions of such a rural paradise simply a fantasy of great wealth? Has the city man thus dreaming the cash to buy a farm or the endurance to run it? However fascinating the visions of rural contentment may be, they are harmful to the city for they divert the city man from an absorption in city affairs. We must be in the city and of the city; its enthusiastic partisans. Absorption in such an interest would go far toward making the city perfect as an environment for intellectual and spiritual accomplishment.

Anyone who has travelled in New England and has seen the hill towns and the people there knows that there is good reason for leaving them. One sees that the best of the old stock has departed to reap the opportunity for independence and a career which only the city offers. There are left on the old farms only the weak of will, the indolent and the moron.

It appears to me that city people enjoy better health, live longer and are more intelligent than country people, which is what anyone could guess who had seen much of either. To prove it by statistics would be too easy. The healthiest district in the city, judging by recent statements, is one of the most crowded of the East Side.

We do find many original types in the country, where men have been forced by solitude to use their minds and have arrived at their own opinions of many things. In the country there may be a less parrotlike repetition of the same phrases, which we of the city pick up so readily from the newspapers.

Life in the country has its charms—it is pleasant to feel moist, springy earth under one's feet, to feel the air always stirring, to hear the sounds of multitudinous life. Few know this better than I, but I know, too, the dulling hard labor, the work that is never done, the envy and spite of neighbors too well known, the constant fight against minor difficulties of wind and weather, the lack of companionship and amusement, of opportunity for advancement. What after all can rural life have to offer in comparison with city life? Few endure it in contentment if they cannot often get to some city.

Is the city any further from Nature than the country? The same wind blows in from the open sea whether we be at the Battery or at Montauk Point. Is spring ever so lovely as in the park where one can enjoy it to the utmost and walk dry shod? The sun shines on city as on country, and moon and stars are the same. Would not a little more park and a few weeks vacation to revel in the sensual delights of the country satisfy us completely? We have simply in our haste and carelessness forgotten to make the city beautiful, as a city. But that is an error which can be righted, and we shall then with our own great Whitman sing the glories of the city.

"Ah, what can ever be more stately and admirable to me than mast-hemmed Manhattan?"

Conservative people contemplating modern improvements and machines are always wondering why people like them and they seem hurt when trolley cars, subways and railroads become popular, for it offends their rationalistic notions.

It seems to hurt those possessed of urbaphobia to see vacant land in Queens and Nassau Counties, and they would at once like to distribute the whole population of New York City evenly over a larger territory. But to what advantage? Can they not see that soon these counties will be as densely built as New York? That the present too great dilution there will give way to a rich density like Manhattan? Is it going too far to say that cities are the clotted cream of the population?

It is impertinent to suggest that there is waste in hauling people back and forth in the city, for that is only to be judged from the point of view. If I wish to live in Nassau County and find it to my advantage to work in Manhattan, shall someone order me to move or change my job? Or say that I waste my time in travelling? Who knows whether it is a waste for me or not?

We must not rail at the congestion of the city while enjoying its advantages. To say, "wouldn't it be nice if there were fewer people" is to wish it away, or to wish for a special license to enjoy it alone without the annoyance of others having an equal right in the same enjoyment, for it would not exist with fewer people. Congestion is an indispensable condition of the pleasure, ease and convenience of the city.

If we enjoy the department store with its treasures collected from all the world, we must realize that it is not there for us alone, that without our million or so neighbors and many guests it could not be there. So it is with all the other things, churches, museums, lectures, music, exhibitions, taxicabs and subways.

It would be easy to show how diffusion defeats its ends and brings greater hardships, for it means inevitably more time lost in travel; more money spent for which the return is to be found only in more space and diminished opportunity. Any plan whereby every worker in office, in shop and factory, could walk to his work, would entail endless labor of worktime travel, of truckage, of annoyance, and how could such a plan be stabilized? Would anyone care to live in such a mixed district? Our tendency, still vigorously fought by some city planners, is all toward a separation of work and home, which is the chief reason for zoning, yet zoning will not satisfy the dilutionists.[21]

Though rents go up with each increase of population, yet the rent becomes more worth paying because opportunities of every sort keep pace also with the population. It is never mere cheapness of living that determines a man's residence, or we should all be in the tropics. It would not be difficult, I think, to show that cheap living means low wages, dear living high wages, the ratio between the cheap and low and the dear and high being nearly the same. But the advantage is all in favor of the high wages and the dear living, for this combination means greater opportunity and an enormous amount of free things which are the result of communal enterprise. It is true that rents are high in New York, but living on the whole is cheaper if by living we mean anything more than minimum necessities. Some of the luxuries of life are to be included in minimum necessities. Without some intellectual stimulation, some pleasure, life is not worth living. A minimum wage based on mere decent living offers in the city a thousand opportunities for delight. A minimum wage in the country offers nothing except food, clothing, a roof and the hooting owls. In New York we get so much for which we do not pay directly. It is thrown in with the rent. Nor do New Yorkers need to have much money invested in homes or furniture or tools.

The city offers the only opportunity for special talents whether it be the making of mouse traps as suggested by Emerson or the repair of teething rings. A genius for playing the harmonica, or the celesta, or for tricks of skill, strength, endurance or contortion will secure a man a good livelihood in the city, but in the country what audience can one collect for a glockenspiel concert?

It is all too easy to give one's enthusiasm rein and become extravagant in imagining the perfect equipment of the big city, yet if it serve to put before us vividly the infinite possibilities of enterprises undertaken in common and paid for out of taxes, or fees without profit, the extravagance of our thought may be justifiable.

I have calculated for instance that if New York were as well equipped as Hartford, Conn. with facilities for public recreation it would require

1000 Baseball diamonds
800 Tennis courts
240 Football fields
80 Outdoor gymnasiums
40 18 hole golf courses

120 Bowling greens
80 Outdoor basket ball courts.

There are many other recreational facilities for games, for exercise, and for sport which should be found in a big city. Americans have never favored public horse races or steeple chases, yet they are common in Europe. The base-ball game seems to take the place of the Latin bull fight, but we might have the stadium or colosseum or amphitheatre for other enterprises or amusements.

Increasing population pushing the suburbs and the country further away, makes it necessary to use our parks and squares more intelligently and more intensively. The demand for children's playgrounds now that the streets are crowded with motor cars is more and more insistent and must be met in new ways if necessary.

VI

A THOUSAND OR MORE THINGS are necessary for the continued growth and prosperity of a big city, any one of which in the opinion of experts is sufficient to limit it to its present size. This has always been the opinion of experts but cities continue to grow. The many factors influencing the city's growth cannot be discussed here in detail, but few of them will seem unsurmountable if we give them thought. Fire has ceased to be a bar to growth in most cities. They are practically unburnable. Earthquakes may forever limit the congestion per acre (that is in tall buildings and multifamily houses) in many regions but they will not retard the limitless spread of cities over the country side. New York seems free from this danger, although a too enthusiastic scientist said a year ago that the surface was overloaded by tall buildings. Scientists make mistakes and this one had forgotten that the earth and rock taken from the deep cellars weighed more than most of the buildings. Subways and gas pipes certainly lighten the load.

Water is the great necessity of city life. Some people have said that the unlimited growth of the city and its increasing demand for water might be a stumbling block in the near future. It is hard to believe that there is any danger from that source for water is one of the indestructible materials. It can be used, purified and used again and again ad infinitum. It falls here at the rate of about thirty-six inches a year and most of that enormous supply is wasted but can be saved and stored for future use. The run off from agricultural lands can be used if it is filtered or if crops and cattle are kept a little distance from the streams. Storing and carrying this water to the city may be expensive but no more so than our present supply. If more water is needed it can be procured and paid for. The imagination which is appalled by the quantity of water we use and the distance it is brought is in constant danger of overstrain but I suppose people have always been so. The marvel of today is a commonplace thing of tomorrow.

We are wasteful of water which is a fault easy to correct by installing meters, by requiring better plumbing more economical in the use of water and by restricting its waste in manufacturing. Manufacturers can recover water for use again without great difficulty, but seldom do so because it has been so cheap. A secondary supply might easily be provided for manufacturing if the supply for household use becomes insufficient. Unlimited possibilities for water like those of New York are not given to every city. Many of them have poor water and can never get it in sufficient quantity to permit an unrestricted growth, because the water is not there. Many middle western towns and many places in the south may be so limited in the future.

The next indispensable requirement of the city is food, which has been a stumbling block for many students.

I would not care to make the consideration of this problem appear simple, for it is complicated beyond all others, and has been more studied than most city problems. The studies that have been made however lack an exact scientific basis and are for the most part guesses, inferences, deductions, from the known habits of certain races. It is complicated by the Malthusian fear of over population, by theories of diet, and by notions of every kind.

We have only to remember the habitual diet of the hardy Eskimo, or of the powerful Asiatic, Tartar, or Arab, to realize that human requirements are variable and not to be fixed by European standards. Habits of diet can be changed without altering strength, endurance or expectation of life. Failure to reckon with this fact invalidates most speculation about food supplies.

The second error in all estimates and speculations is that no one knows as a matter of demonstrable fact what the maximum production per acre may be. In Belgium it is said to be, of wheat, thirty bushels per acre. In the United States it averages about twelve. If we can reach the Belgian standard, we have provided for 250 million people on our present acreage in cultivation. We might easily surpass it, for the investigations of chemists, bacteriologists and agriculturists will certainly show us how. That we do not produce more is because it does not pay, and it will not pay so long as a surplus is so easily raised by our present inexpensive methods.

Other factors in the problem which are still unknown are the possible area of the earth which can be used for agriculture. Wheat fields all over the world have been abandoned ever since the opening of our great west, but if the price goes up little by little and remains up, we shall see many thousands of acres of these fields planted again in wheat. The enormous territory of Russia is largely undeveloped but will some day be brought into the usable part of the world.

Even China where farms abound can be reorganized, and made to double or treble its production, The tropics of course will not produce wheat; but the immense territory in South America, in Africa, and in Asia can be made to yield other starchy foods, which will be accepted instead of wheat in many parts of the world.

In the United States the same relation exists between the price of wheat and area of land in cultivation. For higher prices it will pay to cultivate land, not so advantageous in soil moisture, topography, or situation which is wild or used for grazing today.

The danger of a shortage of food when such a large part of the earth is unproductive or under productive in these days of easy transportation seems too remote to cause any concern.

Our methods of preserving food in cans or in cold storage though often condemned seem to stand the test of use, however unwise they may be in theory, and they add immeasurably to our capacity to feed ourselves.

There is in all these problems a human element which removes them from the consideration of a scientific study by courtesy called exact. Human habits may change so that the kind, quality, and quantity of food may be in a hundred years entirely different from what it is today. Has it not changed indeed in our memory? The groaning board is no longer fashionable and people who live as they say "off the delicatessen" or in cafeterias achieve no social distinction by the possession or eating of food. When eating is done in secret, a slim diet suffices. In the country it is different.

Pigs and chickens and cattle must be raised and eaten to maintain one's social position. My father's father remembered the time when on the banks of the Connecticut salt shad were eaten in secret because they cost nothing and it was a sign of an empty pork barrel and an improvident farmer to be caught eating shad.

There are so far as I have been able to learn no abandoned cities in this country, although many mining camps once busy and prosperous have been abandoned after the mines have been exhausted or proven worthless. Similar instances in great numbers can be found but so far there are no examples in America of a city once great going to ruin.

Many cities have come near this point but their fortunes have been revived by changing conditions. Salem, Massachusetts was once a thriving and important seaport but declined with the increasing prosperity of Boston and went into a period of decay following the change to steamships. Its shipping is of no importance today yet Salem grows because of manufacturing and because it is at last a suburb of Boston. New Bedford, once a seafaring town, has found a new youth in cotton and other industries. Portsmouth, New Hampshire and some of the Maine ports have declined in population and commerce but find a new prosperity as summer resorts.

The manufacturers of the Naugatuck Valley[22] and of other places in New England, as I have already suggested, may some day find their competitors in other cities doing more business and they may be compelled to move or fail. The reason for their first prosperity being water power and that advantage having passed, they find themselves badly located. The reluctance of workers to pull up stakes and move on to a new location is probably the only reason they have not started already to decline.

The Naugatuck Valley is an interesting case when compared with the Housatonic only a few miles away and parallel with it. The Naugatuck power was small, easily developed and therefore attractive to early manufacturers while the Housatonic was large, expensive to develop, and therefore left alone. The Naugatuck Valley has a large population with considerable cities (Derby, Ansonia, Naugatuck, Waterbury, Torrington, Winsted) whereas there are no considerable towns on the Housatonic above Derby.

Today the Housatonic power is largely developed by the dams at Canaan, Kent, a new one below New Milford and at Stephenson, but the power is all electrically transported to the Naugatuck Valley and beyond. There is no reason to suppose that there will ever be manufacturing or sizable towns in the valley of the Housatonic. This nearby water power development may for a time stay the decline of the Naugatuck district.

Many towns are feeling the results of the diminishing railway traffic and their people are looking toward the big city as a more favorable location. Centers which were once important do little business. Last year the Boston and Maine Railroad asked permission to abandon more than a thousand miles of track, much of it short branches to little towns which are better served by automobiles or which have themselves declined because of the concentration of people in big cities.

There may be many important towns or cities in the middle west which will grow no more. They will possibly be held to their present size, by special industries which cannot move, by farming, by inertia for a time, but they must in the end give in to the tide of industry which sweeps toward the big cities but more especially to that narrow strip between the eastern seaboard and the mountains. Lying between sea and coal and being excellently well served by water power electrically transported, this region will ultimately contain more than half and perhaps three quarters of the people of the United States.

Other coal fields may be developed and other places may be advantageous like the Great Lakes basin for instance, but there is small hope of finding great cities in territory away from coal and where the only industry is agricultural.

The sudden prosperity of cotton mills in the south is owing more to cheap living and cheap labor than to any superiority of the location for cotton spinning and weaving. Labor which is cheap because it has heretofore been unemployed is an uncertain foundation for industrial development.

Many city troubles of the present seem inconsequential and temporary, and among these are the annoyances due to our over-burdened railroad freight terminals, for it is even now proposed by the Port Authority to end this in New York by means of freight classification yards and narrow gauge freight subways. In time all terminals must be abolished. Freight will be delivered in carloads to big factories, in small trains to small factories, or be unloaded from car to motor truck and hauled to destination.

The greatest annoyance in cities today is that our highways inherited from a horse drawn age seem insufficient for our present needs. To rebuild an entire city to meet the requirements of such an epoch-making device as the motor car, has been thought of by many city planners, but as E.P. Goodrich says "all that is required is a better use of street space without resort to grandiose schemes and financially impossible new arteries."[23] The approach to the problem, however, must be a new one. The experience of the past avails nothing. The ideal to be sought is a direct route from the garage in the cellar of my house, with little control or traffic regulation, in any direction to the open country. If we can reach the country easily, the city becomes perfect. We may then live in comfort and gregariously and yet have all the pleasures of rural life. The problem obviously requires a separation of classes of traffic, and the elimination of many grade crossings of streets on trunk highways.

The tendency is strong to dwell on the things in which we are backward, such as highways and to forget our great accomplishments of which water and light are perhaps the greatest. New York has probably the finest water supply in the world, yet it costs something less than fifteen dollars per year for one family in a large house. In the country a good supply is hard to find, expensive to get and costly to maintain. It might easily represent a capital expenditure of $10,000 and cost several hundred dollars a year to operate, plus interest on the investment. Water is the great example of the advantage of living in a large community, but schools and streets and parks are just as good illustrations. It is conservative to say that for each hour spent in a park it costs the New Yorker less than one mill.[24]

It would be hard for an outsider seeing the low cost of

our common enterprises to believe that we do not yet have central heating plants, but that each house has its own fire which must be stoked and have coal brought for it and the ashes taken away.

For a nickel we ride from furthest Brooklyn to uppermost Bronx, roughly twenty miles. Where else in the world can one ride so cheaply? The comfort and convenience of city life is the direct result of its great congestion. Congestion is the life of the city. Reduce it below a certain point and much of our ease and convenience disappears. That it is overdone, that our comfortable subways are uncomfortably crowded, is only a temporary condition due to faulty political machinery. We have seen every mode of transportation hailed as the great cure of our transportation ills; have seen it become crowded and have seen the crowd thin out with the building of new lines.

We are certain in the future, I think, to have great cities thinning out quickly into suburbs, a few farming districts scattered here and there on the best land where all work is done by machine, numerous golf clubs as nuclei for suburban communities, but at places touching the city there may be forest in which the deer and bear and even perhaps the wolf will roam.

In my lifetime I have seen the decrease of rural population. Thirty years ago I had never seen a wild deer and one had to go to the Adirondacks or Canada or Maine to get one. Today I could, if I were skilful, see one in half an hour's motor trip from the City to Westchester, Connecticut or New Jersey. Our concentration in cities and the desertion of the country brings us nearer the wilderness than ever and it is infinitely less labor to get there.

Colonel W. J. Wilgus in his valuable study "Transportation in the New York Region," considers all transportation whether by water, railroad, or highway, of goods and people.

The plan proposes a complete reorganization of railroad tracks and terminals throughout the region. They will be arranged so that freight which now passes through the city will go around it on one of two belt lines. Less than carload freight will be handled in freight subways from the railroad yard to its destination at the door of the consignee. Many passenger terminals are proposed giving a better distribution and greater convenience especially when linked with the unified suburban rapid transit system as proposed by D. L. Turner.[25]

More startling though no more revolutionary is the proposal to run a causeway from Rockaway Point to Sandy Hook, thus enclosing the lower bay except for an opening at the channel where the railroads and highways would be carried under the channel in tunnels.

This causeway besides giving a location for the belt-line railway and highway will provide many miles of new beach and seaside parks, which, because of the intimate relation of railway and highway and beach will be easily accessible to all in the region.

Filling in parts of the lower bay to provide more land for parks or for industrial and business or residential use, though not considered in the report will be a natural sequence of building the causeway.

As Colonel Wilgus says in his summary, unification of all transportation and planning for transportation in the whole area is the only hope and to deny the possibility of this is to deny our capacity for self government. As the railroad is the cause of our great city, it is clearly the function of the city to control the railroad in order that its reasonable and healthy growth be not interfered with. Colonel Wilgus' studies set us a long way forward to the time of unified control, for he has the vision to see that all these things have a valuable by-product in usable space, in reduction of cost, in greater convenience and in the individual's liberty to pursue health and happiness which justifies their great cost.

Statistics are always impressive but unconvincing, yet we must find some way to prove to several million people that the saving of a few dollars here and a few dollars there, in the cost of handling their food, necessary clothes, building material and other supplies will more than pay for this colossal undertaking. If my cost of living can be reduced by ten dollars a year on freight and haulage, it is a fair inference that the same thing can be done for ten million people, making a grand total of $100,000,000 for improvements.

The plan follows the latest ideas of city planning in that it seeks to distribute the population evenly over the entire area. This is accomplished by giving transportation to districts which are now without it and by giving equal ease of communication to all districts thus ending the chief cause of our troubles, which is the superior convenience of certain districts, due to the shape of our little island. When it ceases to be an island and all outlying territory is equally desirable for residence and for business, we shall have (given the initial concentration of twenty million people) a distribution and decentralization based upon the common desire for more agreeable surroundings, rather than a concentration dependent upon convenience of access to work as is the case at present.

There will then be no open fields surrounded by densely built sections, but a uniform distribution over the whole area, and new buildings, it is to be expected, will be evenly spread around the edges of the city. The tendency of this more diffuse growth will be a stabilization of values throughout the territory, and the beneficial concentration of more people in the territory.

VII

I T IS EASY FOR AN AMATEUR to sit down before a blank piece of paper and with the help of a book of statistics figure the population of the world in the year 2000 or 2500 or any intermediate year. If the paper holds out, the result is sure to be terrifying, and the gentle reformer is faced by the prospect of having more people in the world than he thinks it can support. He may, so he thinks, be forced to give up for that reason some of the luxuries he now enjoys, and fearing perhaps hand to hand encounters for a crust of bread, he resolves that propagation of the human species must be stopped before this catastrophe can happen. The more careful studies of biologists do not give such alarming results.

I have attempted to show how many things can be done to produce food in an abundance which when we figure it up, is as appalling as the growth of cities, or of population. It is necessary only to suggest the influences determining the increase of population in order to make us feel sure that food and people will always be in a fixed relation, that is, sufficient food for all, and to make us forget the Malthusian fear of over-population.

That people have starved and may starve again before the majority are gathered into the cities is not denied, but it is not proof that the world can be over-populated. There are no modern cities in the parts of the world subject to famine and the circumstances which make the big city possible will prevent the recurrence of famine. We cannot have famine in New York or London or Paris because the agriculture of the whole world cannot be all destroyed at once. Such starvation as we have is due to the present imperfect organization of city living, to accident or to the inferiority of the individual. It is in no case to be blamed on the city which is the seat of abundance.

Without Birth Control Leagues, without propaganda, the increase of population is yet controlled. As a famous sociologist says "when children cease to be assets (as they were before child labor laws and are today on the farm) and become liabilities, they are reduced in number by the wish of parents." The desire to bring children up well, to give them an education and opportunities for ease and advancement will always be a tendency toward small families. Reluctance to divide an estate into many portions, the interests of women outside the home, and the absorption of men in business are well recognized reasons for small families. Part of the world is free from such controlling factors and propagates itself without restraint, but as people fall under the sway of modern conditions, become urbanized, industrialized and standardized, they wait longer to marry and do not have so many children.

There will undoubtedly arise in the cities a new standard of human capacity so that the low mentality will hesitate to reproduce itself, well knowing that its offspring will be morons, quickly discovered and outclassed in the competitive life of the city. Halfwits and morons are easily employed, easily hidden and bring little disgrace in the country, but in the city they and their parents have a hard time.

Statistics of the past prove nothing about the changing conditions of today and tomorrow. Indeed the whole question is chaotic. We hear first of a declining population in France, perhaps the most urbanized and civilized country, and of attempts to stimulate its increase. Then we learn that our college graduates have few children and race suicide becomes an issue; next that the population of the world must be controlled before it becomes impossible to feed it.

The quality of the urbanized race is often attacked but there is nothing to show that we are not improving. We have surpassed all feats of strength, speed and endurance known to the ancient Greeks and there are no tricks in which we have failed to surpass our own adored Indian. We are, so far as we can judge, a little better in physique than our forebears of any age, and our judgment in this is more to be trusted than the studies of biologists whose statistics go back only a generation or two; which is a mere nothing in the millions of generations that have passed and are to come.

Parturition and lactation have not changed in spite of alarmists and a woman can be as good a mother in the city as in the country.[26] Such fundamental characteristics as those of bearing and rearing children cannot be changed in a few generations and there is no reliable information to show that any change whatever is taking place in our physical capacity or in our attitude toward living. The eccentricities of a few individuals do not change the qualities which they transmit from their ancestors to their offspring.

There are many social and ethical advances due to the herding in cities, but I prefer to call it a congregation rather than a herd. If there be merit in the self-discipline required by regularity of habits, by punctuality, by industry, it is to be found in the city to a greater degree than in the country. Time for the true countryman means nothing, whether it be his time or another's, and most of his work can be better done tomorrow than today. Idlers and wastrels are alike the world over, but those of the city are not in greater proportion or more expert than those of the country. I have seen the snaky head of vice in the city and country, but never has it seemed so cruel or so abhorrent as in the country.

City people, I think, are less irritated by each other, less jealous and envious, for they have more chances for comparison, more opportunities to avoid unpleasant encounters. The feelings of city people are less hurt by differences in standards of living.

There is among the people of New York a comfortable tolerance and in a crowd ill-humor and irritation are rare. I suspect that those who show great annoyance in the subway are visitors from the solitudes, little accustomed to people and only at home in the out-of-doors.

I believe, too, that city people are many of them inspired to an industry unknown in the country and that they work because they wish to rather than because they must. To be part of a big organization has a thrill of its own for many who would lack that incentive on a farm.

We have as yet in the city only touched the surface of living. We have brought to the city country habits and unrecognized desires for ease and sensual delights which are out of harmony or in themselves childish. Our small parks are still supposed to be little bits of rural scenery on exhibition in the city instead of being, as they should be, like hot houses with living things to delight the senses but in an environment wholly artificial.

Of real freedom to follow an interest or a hobby the great city gives more and more in proportion to its greatness. Individuality does not consist in eccentricities of demeanor, or dress, like going with or without hat or shoes, yet such foolishness can be indulged more freely in the great city than in a small village. The trouble is that individuality is so rare and always has been. The opportunities for its growth were never better than today, can never be better than in the great city where as compared with the country or with the past so little is needed to provide for mere existence, and there is so much time which the individual can use as his desires indicate.

I have seen a man plough and plant and cultivate a field. Round and round he goes hour after hour, day after day, condemned as it were to four months hard labor in 40 acres of corn or tobacco. It seems more dulling to intellect and to individuality than running a machine in a factory; the cruel sun overhead, the choking dust and the exhausting toil are not made much pleasanter by the singing birds and burrowing woodchucks. People worry about the use we shall make of our leisure, which is always increasing as the working day gets shorter, but this is a materialistic worry which sees in leisure only time taken from money-making work; a lost opportunity to produce some object. That one should by the use of leisure produce an idea, a philosophy, a mode of life, is inconceivable to these materialists, and doubtless such effort has no value to them.

The idea of questioning increasing leisure for fear people will not know what to do with it is as silly as questioning other forms of wealth of which this is the greatest. But the true test of the use of leisure is the intellect which uses it; for some leisure may not have great value but I doubt if it is more harmful to society than their other activities.

If the merry populace have time to dance and sing, why should we object? Surely it is a happier state than that of the serf working sixteen hours for a bare existence, always miserable, without hope and without charity in his heart. I believe the dark ages of unwilling hard labor are gone, and that the friendly light of the city will continue to shine through the ages, calling people to come to communion with their fellows.

The industrialization of city people will undoubtedly bring about a number of difficulties. The problem is so vast and is complicated by so many factors difficult to measure in their influence that the mind is reluctant to undertake its solution.

Business of every kind has felt the stimulation of the machine and could not be carried on, at the present scale without machines. Every new office machine has as a concomitant, a machine in the factory producing more than before. Each machine handles, as we might say, the product of the other; one manufacturing, the other writing orders, or calculating, or billing, the order.

The city must be in future as in the past the great field

for the machine, and the machine means quantity whether it be transportation or pins, and from this quantity production we shall all reap benefit in cheapness, ease and comfort of living.

To speculate about the development in one direction or another is too easy to be entertaining. One has only to indicate the direction and any one can go. It is sufficient to point out that some ten car subway trains are now operated by two guards and a motor-man. Cheap power has quite obvious consequences.

Our capacity to buy all kinds of goods seems unlimited. Anything which is cheaper, or better or more luxurious can be sold, in almost unlimited amounts, yet the time may come when the products cannot all be marketed and the making must be curtailed. It is reasonable to expect then, not a reduction in the number of workers but a reduction in the number of hours per day which each one works. The reduction in the number of hours of work will ultimately be the most beneficent result of industrialism. The public will continue to support the shorter work day, in future, as it has on many occasions in the past. Increasing leisure will bring many difficulties, but it may be the cause of a revival of the crafts, and perhaps of the arts. It seems reasonable to me to think that a man who tends a machine for six hours or less will have some energy left for creative work which he will use in making for himself by hand some of the things which he cannot afford to buy. Minds of another kind will be occupied with creative work in society, in the church or in intellectual pursuits.

We are entering the golden age of the avocation. I cannot believe that the reduced working day will much reduce the scale of living of the workers or that the universal machines will free many of them for service as lackeys. It seems unlikely that we shall ever have in this country the servant class which was so large a proportion of the English people. They are being freed even there by the machines.

In the country people can afford none or only a small machine but any machine (as a subway for instance) can be profitably used in the city. The more people, the more laborsaving machinery we can have. It may be that we are only at the beginning of the era of the machine.

The city is the great example of quantity production, whether it be transportation or parks. For our parks considered as a factory to produce, turn out millions of pleasurable hours per person per day at an infinitesimal cost per unit of production. It is unsafe to be rational about the city. We cannot establish certain premises and argue from them to a rational conclusion, for the premises may be unsound and the conclusion be proven futile before we can get our theory worked out. We must in everything be empirical and ask of every condition and of every plan, what possible difference is it likely to make in future?

If, however, we choose to rationalize about the city and choose to push to its furthest limits in imagination the concentration of people in a small space; their standardization so-called; their full dependence upon machinery and their submission to an industrial discipline, we should dare to start with the hypothesis that the city is wholly good. We should dare also to disregard the sensuous appeal of the country and consider whether the heightened pleasure of the city man in the country is not in the end more productive emotionally than the constant presence of rural nature is to the country man.

We should consider too whether rural delights are actually cut off from city people; whether in short nature is not as charming in the city as in the country and whether city delights, which are impossible in the country do not make up for the solitary enjoyment of an unpeopled wilderness. Not many people have tried varying Thoreau's experiment at Walden to see how little space they could live in comfortably and decently in the city; or what beans may be made to grow and what arrowheads picked up on city streets. There is no solitude so perfect as that of the city (when one is in one's own little corner) and nowhere in the world that one can be so indifferent and so unconscious of one's fellows.

It cannot be proven that a certain attitude of mind toward one thing or another in our environment is essential to wellbeing either physical or mental. The sea murmurs to the sailor words that he loves and understands; but to the mountaineer accustomed to the silence of deep snows, the noise of the sea is futile and irritating excitement. The countryman is at home in the woods and fields and is distressed by the roar and the apparent disorder of the city, while the city man in the country hears the cock crow through the night but in the city sleeps through the sweet noises made by milkman and roisterer. Which by this test is the better man?

Campers and sailors go on long voyages with almost no duffle, they have only a bunk of their own or only a shelter for their heads in a vast wilderness. Must city people on a voyage perhaps no longer occupy so much space? Can it be after all that we are actually prodigal of space and have everywhere streets too wide, rooms too large and carry with us too many cumbers? Who will be the prophet and the genius of the city and build more stately mansions and more convenient kitchenettes?

THE END

Notes

Introduction: The Necessity for Congestion

1. Theodora Kimball Hubbard, review of Lay, *The Freedom of the City* by Charles D. Lay, *City Planning* 2:4 (October, 1926), 308.

2. Charles Downing Lay, *The Freedom of the City* (New York: Duffield & Company, 1926), 49, 99.

3. Lay, *Freedom of the City*, 84.

4. Lay, *Freedom of the City*, 46, 64–65, 82.

5. Lewis Mumford, "Up at a Villa—Down in the City," *The New Republic* (October 27, 1926). The title refers to a famous poem by Robert Browning.

6. Henry James Forman, "To Be or Not to Be A Citizen: Contradictory Virtues of City and Country Living," *New York Times* (20 June, 1926).

7. Lay, *Freedom of the City*, 24.

8. "Cockneys and Clodhoppers," *Christian Science Monitor* (June 16, 1926).

9. Lay, *Freedom of the City*, 19.

10. Letter from C. D. Lay to Dr. Rita Morgan, Welfare Council, New York (January 1, 1949), Box 17, Charles Downing Lay Papers, 1898–1956, Division of Rare and Manuscript Collections, Carl A. Kroch Library, Cornell University.

11. Rem Koolhaas, *Delirious New York: A Retroactive Manifesto for Manhattan* (New York: Oxford University Press, 1978), 15; Koolhaas, "Life in the Metropolis' or 'The Culture of Congestion'," *Architectural Design* 5 (1977), 320.

12. Vicki Been, "City NIMBYs," *Journal of Land Use* 33:2, 218.

13. William A. Fischel, *The Homevoter Hypothesis* (Cambridge: Harvard University Press, 2001), 18.

14. See Richard Florida, *The New Urban Crisis* (New York: Basic Books, 2017), 64–65.

15. Been, "City NIMBYs," 221.

16. Edward Glaeser, "Houston, New York Has a Problem," *City Journal* (Summer 2008).

17. Nolan Gray, "Abolish Zoning—All of It," *Reason* (June 21, 2022).

18. Been, "City NIMBYs," 231–232.

19. Jonathan T. Rothwell, "Racial Enclaves and Density Zoning: The Institutionalized Segregation of Racial Minorities in the United States," *American Law and Economics Review* 13:1 (Spring 2011), 291

20. Frederick Hoppin to C. D. Lay (20 November, 1925); Horace Green to Lay (November 25, 1925); Lay to Green (1 December, 1925); Lay to Green (17 February, 1926); David T. Walden to Lay (March 23, 1926), Charles Downing Lay Papers, 1898–1956, Division of Rare and Manuscript Collections, Carl A. Kroch Library, Cornell University.

21. Forman, "To Be or Not To Be"

The Life and Work of Charles Downing Lay

1. "Charles Downing Lay First American to Win Olympic Medal," *York Daily Record* (August 1, 1936).

2. In 1909, Langton committed suicide by downing a bottle of potassium cyanide. He was just 50 years old and left behind two children and his wife, Berenice, a sculptor who had studied with Rodin and Saint-Gaudens. Langton's successor at the Hudson County Park Commission was Charles N. Lowrie.

3. Mahonri Young's daughter Agnes would marry Lay's son Oliver many years later.

4. O. R. Pilat, "Most Versatile Is Lay, Marine Park Planner," *Brooklyn Daily Eagle* (July 13, 1931).

5. Letter from Charles D. Lay to Henry V. Hubbard (February 7, 1910), Charles Downing Lay Papers, PR366, Box 1, New-York Historical Society.

6. "Lay Says Disorder Reigns in the Park," *New-York Tribune* (August 22, 1911).

7. "Disorder Reigns," *New-York Tribune* (August 22, 1911); "Will Remodel Battery," *New-York Tribune* (March 18, 1912); "Park Report Withheld," *New-York Tribune* (January 28, 1912); "Lay Vetoed Frick Offer," *New-York Tribune* (June 28, 1912).

8. "Disagrees with Mayor," *New-York Tribune* (October 28, 1911); "Spurns Gaynor Advice and a Park Board Job," *New-York Tribune* (May 2, 1913); Letter from Charles D. Lay to Park Board (May 1, 1913), Charles Downing Lay Papers, 1898–1956, Division of Rare and Manuscript Collections, Carl A. Kroch Library, Cornell University.

9. "Pestless Japanese Trees Coming Here," *New York Times* (January 30, 1910); "Cherry Trees on the Way," *New-York Tribune* (March 6, 1912); "Cherry Tree Tablet Accepted by City," *New York Times* (April 29, 1912).

The Lay plan was erased in 1932 for a more formal design by the Olmsted Brothers.

10. Charles D. Lay, "Some Opinions About Landscape Design," *Landscape Architecture* 20:4 (July 1930).

11. Letter from Charles D. Lay to Robert Wheelwright (January 27, 1927), Charles D. Lay and Lay family papers, Archives of American Art, Smithsonian Institution.

12. Diana Rice, "This Garden Belongs to the Children," *New York Times* (December 4, 1927). Vonnoh's piece was cast instead for the Conservatory Garden that Robert Moses built at Fifth Avenue and 105th Street.

13. Charles D. Lay, *A Park System for Long Island: A Report to the Nassau County Committee* (February 1925), 7, 2–3.

14. Lay, *A Park System for Long Island* (February 1925), 9; Letter from Charles D. Lay to Michael J. Kennedy (April 28, 1913), Charles Downing Lay Papers, 1898–1956, Division of Rare and Manuscript Collections, Carl A. Kroch Library, Cornell University.

15. Charles D. Lay, "An Arterial Highway for Long Island" (March 10, 1927), 5, Charles Downing Lay Papers, 1898–1956, Division of Rare and Manuscript Collections, Carl A. Kroch Library, Cornell University.

16. Lay, *A Park System for Long Island*, 10.

17. Lay, *A Park System for Long Island*, 5; Robert Moses quoted in Marshall Berman, *All That is Solid Melts into Air: The Experience of Modernity* (Penguin Books, 1982), 301.

18. Charles D. Lay, "Rush of Prospective Home-Owners for Land Along the Housatonic Foreseen by Landscape Architect," *Milford News* (September 1, 1944).

19. "Post War Planning Board Studying Projects Including Plans for Housatonic Motor Drive and Shore Parkway," *Bridgeport Post* (September 3, 1944).

20. "Scenic Parkway Along Housatonic Proposed in Bill," *Newtown Bee* (February 2, 1945).

21. Letter from Robert Moses to Charles D. Lay (April 28, 1922); Charles Downing Lay Papers, 1898–1956, Division of Rare and Manuscript Collections, Carl A. Kroch Library, Cornell University.

22. "Park Commissioner Browne Proposes 30 to 50 Millions Expenditure on Elaborate Layout of Marine Park," *Brooklyn Daily Eagle* (January 1, 1928).

23. Charles Downing Lay, "Tidal Marshes," *Landscape Architecture* 2:3 (April 1912), 101–102.

24. "Lay, Surprise Architect, Has No Park Plans," *Brooklyn Daily Eagle* (March 26, 1931); "Wants Group to Aid Lay on Marine Park," *New York Times* (7 June, 1931); "Plan for Proposed Marine Park Development," *Brooklyn Daily Eagle* (September 24, 1931); "Design Completed for Marine Park," *New York Times* (February 25, 1932); O. R. Pilat, "Marine Park is New Front Door to Boro," *Brooklyn Times-Union* (10 March, 1932); "Huge Stadium Planned," *New York Times* (October 17, 1931).

25. Dominick Cavallo, *Muscles and Morals: Organized Playgrounds and Urban Reform, 1880–1920* (Philadelphia: University of Pennsylvania Press, 1981), 2–4.

26. "A New York Project to Multiply Play Space," *The American City* (December 1927).

27. Galen Cranz, *The Politics of Park Design: A History of Urban Parks in America* (Cambridge: MIT Press, 1982), 62; Charles W. Eliot, "Welfare and Happiness in Works of Landscape Architecture," *Landscape Architecture* 1:3 (April, 1911), 147. Charles D. Lay, "Playground Design," *Landscape Architecture* 2:2 (January 1912), 64; "Marine Park," *Brooklyn Daily Eagle* (March 13, 1932).

28. "All the World's a Studio," *Town and Country* (July 15, 1932).

29. "Huge Marine Park Begun in Brooklyn," *Brooklyn Daily Eagle* (February 17, 1933); "Lack of Material Holding Up Work at Marine Park," *Brooklyn Daily Eagle* (January 14, 1934); Robert A. Caro, *The Power Broker: Robert Moses and the Fall of New York* (New York: Knopf, 1974): 363, 370; Letter from Robert Moses to John A. Hefferman, July 8, 1938, box 97, Robert Moses Papers, Manuscripts and Archives Division, New York Public Library, New York; Letter from Robert Moses to Thomas P. Smith, Jr., July 12, 1940, New York City Parks Department General Files, Municipal Archives, New York, New York.

30. Letter from Charles D. Lay to Franklin D. Roosevelt (July 11, 1939), Charles Downing Lay Papers, 1898–1956, Division of Rare and Manuscript Collections, Carl A. Kroch Library, Cornell University; Eleanor Roosevelt, "My Day," *New York World-Telegram* (April 5, 1939 and May 13, 1939).

31. Andrew Jackson Downing, "Shade Trees in Cities," *The Horticulturalist* 8 (August 1, 1852): 345–347; "An Urban Tree," Charles Downing Lay Papers, 1898–1956, Division of Rare and Manuscript Collections, Carl A. Kroch Library, Cornell University. The essay was later published in the *New York Herald Tribune* (August 5, 1932).

32. Charles D. Lay, "The End of a Man's World," *New-York Tribune* (November 19, 1923); Lay, *A Garden Book for Autumn and Winter* (New York: Duffield & Company, 1924).

33. "A Tame Crow," Charles Downing Lay Papers, 1898–1956, Division of Rare and Manuscript Collections, Carl A. Kroch Library, Cornell University. It is not clear where this essay was published.

34. The address was 95 Chapel Street until the 1960s, when the local post office changed the address to 115 Chapel Street.

35. Charles Downing Lay, "This Old House," unpublished manuscript (nd).

The Freedom of the City

1. The first figure has changed little since; current seating at the 41 Broadway theaters is about 50,490.

2. The current population of the city is 8.4 million, with a total of 20.3 million in the New York metropolitan area.

3. The "interesting experiment" is Sunnyside Gardens, a small garden city prototype in Queens planned by Clarence Stein and Henry Wright and developed by Alexander Bing's City Housing Corporation. It was completed in 1928.

4. The reference here is to Oliver Goldsmith's 1770 poem "The Deserted Village," a lamentation on the impacts of rural enclosure and the depopulation of the English countryside.

5. Lay is referring here to the Metropolitan Opera Company's stillborn 1927 plan to move from its original home at 1411 Broadway to a new building on 57th Street between Eight and Ninth Avenues. An opera house was part of early plans for Rockefeller Center, but the company ultimately relocated to Lincoln Center.

6. Invoked here is New York's first citywide zoning code, the 1916 Zoning Resolution, which set limits to building mass and envelope to protect street-level access to air and sunlight.

7. The population of the New York metropolitan area today is over 20 million, while that of New York, New Jersey and Pennsylvania combined is about 41 million.

8. The 1920s was a period of great outmigration to Brooklyn and Queens, where an unprecedented residential building boom—stoked by a 10-year tax holiday—was underway. See Thomas J. Campanella, *Brooklyn: The Once and Future City* (Princeton: Princeton University Press, 2019), 296–325.

9. Lay is referring here to proposals by Lewis Mumford, Clarence Stein and other members of the Regional Planning Association of America to

create suburban "garden cities" on the model of those proposed by English reformer Ebenezer Howard. Garden cities would fuse the best of urban and rural life in low-density live-work environments close to nature, with none of the pollution and overcrowding of large cities. It has proved an elusive ideal, with most attempts devolving into upscale commuter suburbs. The first such effort in the United States was Forest Hills Gardens in Queens, followed shortly after by nearby Sunnyside Gardens.

10. Nearly all of these business and trade agglomerations are long gone, with the partial exception of Wall Street. The 16-story Architects' Building, where Lay maintained an office for many years, was at 101 Park Avenue. Erected in 1912 for design professionals, it became home to dozens of firms—including venerable McKim, Mead and White. The American Academy of Rome was also headquartered there for more than 50 years. The building was razed in 1979 for a 49-story office tower that uses the same address. See Christopher Gray, "Streetscapes: Readers' Questions," *New York Times* (March 7, 1993) and Ada Louise Huxtable, "A Radical Change on the City's Skyline," *New York Times* (July 22, 1979).

11. See note 12 on the garden city movement.

12. The International City and Regional Planning Conference was held in conjunction with the 17th National Conference on City Planning in April, 1925. At the time Lay was writing, New York's outer boroughs were in the midst of a tremendous building boom, one that churned much of still-rural Brooklyn and Queens into tidy blocks of Tudor-revival homes and apartments. See Campanella, *Brooklyn*, 296–325.

13. Lay's "succession of little cities" would eventually be known as the Boston-to-Washington or BosWash corridor. In 1961, French geographer Jean Gottman introduced an ancient Greek term for a super-city, "megalopolis," into the popular lexicon, describing in detail the great conurbation along the Route 1—Interstate 95 corridor between Boston and Washington. Here, Gottman reasoned, was "the largest and densest concentration of highly paid personnel and higher personal income certainly in North America and probably anywhere in the world." See Gottman, *Megalopolis: The Urbanized Northeastern Seaboard of the United States* (1961).

14. Lay is almost certainly referring here to Edgar Chambless, Alabama-born prophet of the linear city—an urban design he delightfully termed an "earthscraper." His self-published 1910 treatise, *Roadtown*, is a cult classic among infrastructure and urbanism junkies (its shortest chapter, "The Servant Problem in Roadtown," is a single sentence: "There will

be no servant problem in Roadtown, as there will be no need for servants").
See Campanella, *Brooklyn*, 421–423.

15. Sparrows Point was one of the leading centers of steel production in
the world. Its vast Bethlehem mill employed tens of thousands of workers
by the 1940s and produced the steel used in the Golden Gate and George
Washington bridges and much of the armament of the first and second
world wars.

16. See Werner Hegeman, "European City Plans and Their Value to the
American City-Planner," *Landscape Architecture* IV:3 (April, 1914): 89–103.

17. For better or worse, the building of such roads was already underway
in Westchester and Long Island by the mid-1920s, with motor parkways
linking New York to an array of parks and towns north and east of the city.

18. This plea to clean up and modernize New York City's vast park sys-
tem would be undertaken a decade later by Robert Moses. See Robert A.
Caro, *The Power Broker: Robert Moses and the Fall of New York* (New York:
Knopf, 1974), 368–401.

19. Imagine if Lay could see today's Escalade, with its 5,800-pound curb
weight and engine five time the power of a 1925 Cadillac.

20. This vision of industrial agriculture would, of course, become reality
in many parts of rural America.

21. Lay is referring again here to Mumford and fellow advocates of the
"garden city."

22. The Naugatuck Valley straddles portions of Litchfield, New Haven
and Fairfield counties in western Connecticut.

23. Ernest Payson Goodrich was an influential city planner and civil
engineer who did extensive traffic and transportation studies for New York
and other cities, including Nanjing and Bogotá. This quote is from a paper
Goodrich read at the 1925 International City and Regional Planning Conference in New York—"The Influence of Zoning on High Buildings and
Street Traffic"—published in *Planning Problems of Town, City and Region*
(Baltimore: The Norman, Remington Company, 1925), 439–485.

24. A notional currency unit equal to a thousandth of a dollar or a tenth
of a cent.

25. William J. Wilgus, chief engineer of the New York Central Railroad,
was the genius behind Grand Central Station—the great "Terminal City"
that transformed Manhattan. He also pioneered the modern concept of air
rights, recognizing that the unused space above terminal and tracks was
a commodity that could be developed or sold (as he put it, "from the air

would be taken wealth"). The Wilgus "belt line" plan—*Proposed New Railway System for the Transportation and Distribution of Freight by Improved Methods in the City and Port of New York*—was published in 1908.

26. Parturition is a technical term for childbirth, or the process of giving birth to offspring.

Index

Page numbers in *italics* indicate figures. Page numbers in **bold** type indicate tables.

About the Authors

Charles Downing Lay (1877–1956) was a landscape architect, city planner, artist, author, and essayist. Born in the Hudson Valley and raised in New York City, he studied with Frederick Law Olmsted, Jr. at Harvard before taking a leadership post with the New York City Department of Parks. A versatile practitioner, his work ran the gamut from private gardens to plans for the City of Albany, the 1939 World's Fair and the industrial new town of Arvida, Quebec. He was a dedicated environmentalist and founder of the Housatonic Valley Association in Connecticut.

Thomas J. Campanella is Professor of City and Regional Planning at Cornell University and Historian-in-Residence of the New York City Parks Department. He has held Guggenheim and Fulbright fellowships and is a Fellow of the American Academy in Rome. His most recent book, *Brooklyn: The Once and Future City* (2019), was a finalist for the Brendan Gill Prize from the Municipal Arts Society of New York.